D1742295

DESIGN IS DIFFERENCE

agIdeas   Ken Cato

Only those who attempt the absurd will
achieve the impossible. I think it's in my basement...
let me go upstairs and check.
— M.C. Escher —

DESIGN MEDIA PUBLISHING LIMITED

2

Published in 2014 by Design Media Publishing Limited, 20th Floor, Manulife Tower, 196 Electric Road North Point, Hongkong, China

ISBN 978-988-12969-5-5

CREATIVE DIRECTOR AND EDITOR
Luis Coderque

DESIGN
Cato Brand Partners
www.catopartners.com.au

DESIGN ASSISTANTS
Hayden Daniel
William Devereux
Cassandra Downs
Elliot Hutchinson

SUB EDITORS
Kristin McCourtie
Eleni Kaponis
Sam Paverd

CONTRIBUTING WRITER
Dan Formosa

COPY EDITOR
David Webster

DESIGN FOUNDATION
6 Otter Steet
Collingwood
Melbourne Vic 3066 Australia
agIdeas.net

Contents

Look Upstairs

DAN FORMOSA

— Preface —

DAN FORMOSA

Australia is an odd place. I'm saying this coming from the US – so it's just my perspective. It's definitely not a small place – just very far away. There are several "opposites" that can be difficult to get used to. The southern-hemisphere seasons are opposite of my northern-hemisphere sensibilities. Winter in July makes no sense. Nor does Christmas without snow. And the time difference is insane (sorry, a 15 or 16 hour time difference is just impossible to calculate.) You celebrate New Year's Day on the morning of New Year's Eve – at least according to my clock in New York. I'm often not even awake yet.

Someone – I think it was someone at agIdeas – told me that no matter where you live in the world, you don't just casually get to Australia. It is not on the way to anywhere.

Exactly! It's an island. Okay, it's a continent – but it's an island. You don't simply drop in because you are passing by. If you find yourself in Australia, chances are good that Australia was your intended destination. And no matter where in the world you're arriving from, it's a long time to be on an airplane.

Yet land in Melbourne after a silly-long flight, and surprisingly, it's not very different here at all. Everyone speaks English – sort of. People are smiling and happy to see you, whether you know them or not. Conversations are instantly engaging, fun, and effortless.

If you're interested in the topic of design and you're especially lucky, or if you planned well, you'll get to Melbourne in April. Because every year a few thousand people descend on Melbourne for what

I believe to be the world's best, biggest and most impactful design event anywhere. The agIdeas team create a massive gathering of some of the most amazing people I have ever met. I'm not talking about the speakers – although I would certainly include them in that description. I'm talking about everyone, the people at agideas who organise the conference, the volunteer committee who you'll eventually just want to take home with you, the speakers who will tell you inspiring stories about their inspiring lives, and especially, the thousands of people who participate. The event lasts for five days and nights, and I'm pretty sure that during that time Melbourne shows up in satellite images as the brightest spot on planet earth.

Speakers at the conference receive plenty of love and accolades. I believe the reasons the speakers seem so amazing, without doubt, is due to the fact that 1) they start out amazing, and especially 2) they instantly absorb the energy emanating from the amazing people who attend. I know I used "amazing" three times in one sentence, but I mean it.

Now I realise you may just be sitting alone somewhere reading this – but raise your hand if you think design can change the world. Now keep it raised if you think design can improve our quality of life. How about improve healthcare. Entertainment. Day-to-day living. The flow of information. Interpersonal and global relationships. Hand still up? Keep it raised one more time if you think design can assist, at least to some extent, in a move towards world peace.

If your hand is still up then you've probably attended an agIdeas event. Because in this gathering people from many corners of the world align for five wonderful days on a very clear vision. That is, whatever your dream may be, it can be done!

I've been lucky enough to be invited to speak at agIdeas twice in the past few years. The great thing about being an agIdeas speaker is that you meet other speakers who have come from near and far to be part of the event. A discussion can go in minutes from the design of a gazillion-dollar dream-liner jet to the subtleties of Arabic typography, from computer-generated space aliens to dance and choreography, from super-natural photography to the wonders of drawing with chalk on a blackboard. And to the bizarre topic of growing meat cells in a lab as an artistic statement (that topic, maybe not surprising, comes from Australia. I told you it is an odd place.)

But as great as it is to be in the back room mingling with a variety of international super-speakers, there is an urge to go back, among the audience, find an empty seat, sit with everyone attending and soak in that afore-mentioned energy. Because agIdeas is not just about the speakers' stories. There are thousands of great and inspiring stories to be heard throughout the week – and not nearly enough time.

From everyone you meet during this Design Week you'll find that this is a great time to be in design – no matter what segment of design you're in. Communication, fashion, products, architecture, environmental, photography, food, digital, animation and more are all included. And you don't need to be a designer by training – fans of design are also well represented. Professionals from many fields, who believe that design can help them not just in their business ventures but in their accomplishments in life, play an important role and blend easily into the mix. Events and exhibitions are presented that engage the youngest in our community from kindergarten to high school and those dreaming of becoming world design leaders, events for business leaders and of course for designers from all facets of the creative industries from all around the region.

While it's a fun and fantastic event, underneath it all there's also a clear sense that we are not living in a utopia. Real-world problems exist, and real-world problems need to be addressed. What you'll see emanating from just about everyone in Melbourne is that design is not really about the design itself. It's not about the physical or virtual manifestation of the idea, innovation or concept. It's about the effect. It's about the impact, large or small, that design can have on an individual, a group of people, a community and a world.

Design Matters: Melbourne's International Design Week and the agIdeas team who present it definitely have an effect.

KEN CATO

— *Introduction* —

KEN CATO

NEWSTAR DESIGN AWARDS

NEWSTAR DESIGN AWARDS

40

PARTICIPATING STUDIOS

All of Us, UK
Fabrica, Italy
Gnomon School of VFX, USA
Guerrilla Games, The Netherlands
IDEO, USA
Ken Miki & Associates, Japan
MadeThought, UK
Pentagram, UK & USA
Prologue, USA
SeymourPowell, UK
TEAGUE, USA
The Designers Republic, UK

Design students from around Australia and across the globe are invited to submit their best work in 2D, 3D and multimedia. All entries submitted are judged by a panel of respected designers, who select a short list of finalists.

From these, the students whose work is considered to be most outstanding by the Look Upstairs speakers are awarded travelling scholarships, to undertake work experience at their choice of one of the world's most innovative and highly regarded studios or to Fabrica, the research workshop, school and studio established by Benetton, established in 1994. These golden opportunities enable the winning students to gain a practical understanding of the international design industry and make valuable connections for the future.

All of the finalists have their work displayed in a prominent and widely promoted exhibition, as well as being published inside this extraordinary book – where their work is viewed by tens of thousands of visitors from Victoria, interstate and abroad.

Through the Newstar program, emerging designers are encouraged to aspire to the highest standards in their work and are rewarded with opportunities that can provide a vital stimulus to their ambitions.

The works of each of the 40 shortlisted 'new stars' for Look Upstairs are showcased on the following pages.

ERICA BOUCHER

RMIT University

Geralds Bar Stationary
Print Design

DEEP BREATH
A ski mask that allows completely buried avalanche victims to breathe and survive beneath avalanche debris.

Deep Breath Ski Mask
Allows completely buried avalanche victims to breathe

Swinburne University of Technology

TRISTAN BREGA

BILLY BURNS

University of Ballarat

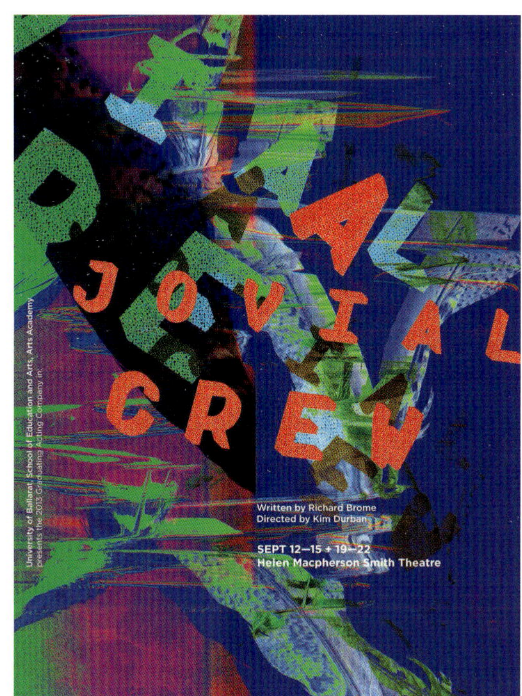

A Jovial Crew
Student Performance
Poster Design

Lily Blacks Bitters
Packaging Design and Identity
Lily Blacks Coctail Bar

Swinburne TAFE

POPPY CALHOUN

KEVIN CHAN

Tunku Abdul Rahman University

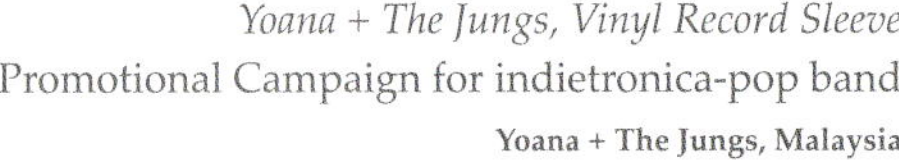

Yoana + The Jungs, Vinyl Record Sleeve
Promotional Campaign for indietronica-pop band
Yoana + The Jungs, Malaysia

Métier Magazine
Craft and Handmade Design Magazine
Publication Design

RMIT University

CARRIE CHILTON

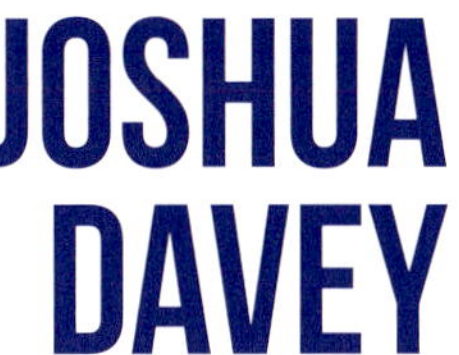

JOSHUA DAVEY

Billy Blue College of Design

Manifesto: You Oppose the Unnatural
Magazine style manifesto, the feminine façade of beauty and societal issues
Publication Design, Essay

Subconsciousness
A3 Poster and A5 Saddle-stich booklet
Photography, Print Design

Swinburne University

JULIAN DE BONO

DAVID EYNAUD

Billy Blue College of Design

ABCDEF
GHIJKLM
NOPQRS
TUVWXYZ

The Creative Joy Project (Custom Typeface)
Professional space for adult creatives with disabilities
Branding Identity & Manifesto

Shelter and Bronze
Branding/Identity Design

RMIT University

AMBER GOEDEGEBUURE

DALE HARDIMAN

RMIT University

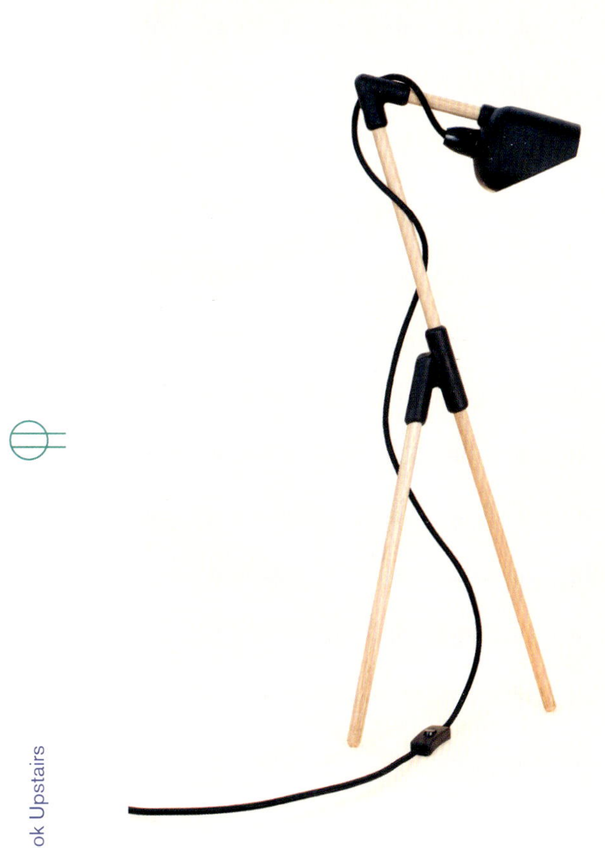

Mr. Dowel Jones
Flat Pack Lamp, rubber and timber components
Commercial Lighting

Mus(ic)cle
Portable speakers, inspired by muscle structures
Cypress Pine

Monash University

MATTHEW HARDING

DAN HENNESSY

University of South Australia

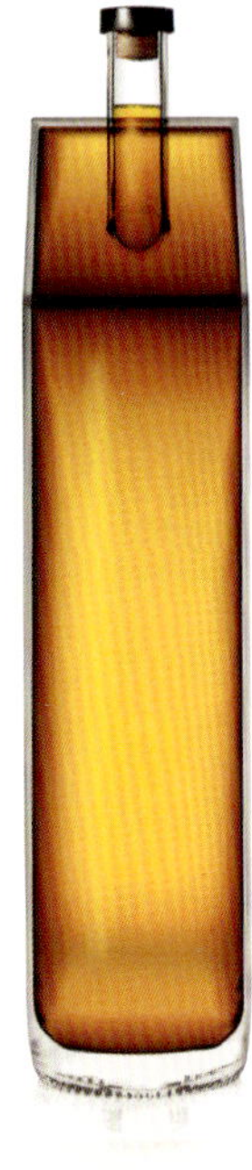

Oriem Scotch Whiskey
Whiskey targeted at the international female consumer
Package Design

Keir Vaughan Brand
Stationery Set, Branding and Identity Design

RMIT Univesirty

STEFAN IMBESI

CAROLINE KAUP

Griffith University

3D Printed & Handcrafted Jewellery
Combining digital craft with handcraft

Archelier Identity
Architecture and Interior Design consultancy
Branding & Identity, Print Design

Parsons School of Design

EDMOND LAU

HOLLY LE

Monash University

Ocean 8
Wine Label and Packaging Design

Natural Fibre Co.
Annual Report and Identity Design

University of South Australia

ARWEN LINDEMANN

JEROME LOUSICK

Billy Blue College of Design

Amplify
Digital hub for Sydney's live music scene
Branding, Print Design

Don't Fuck This Up!
Maze Poster

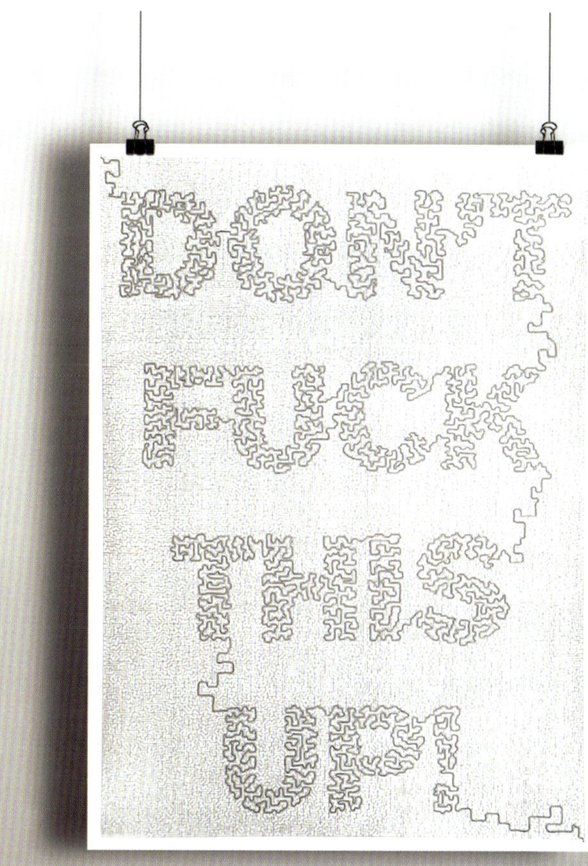

Monash University

JOSHUA MCCORMACK

WILL MCKENZIE

Swinburne University

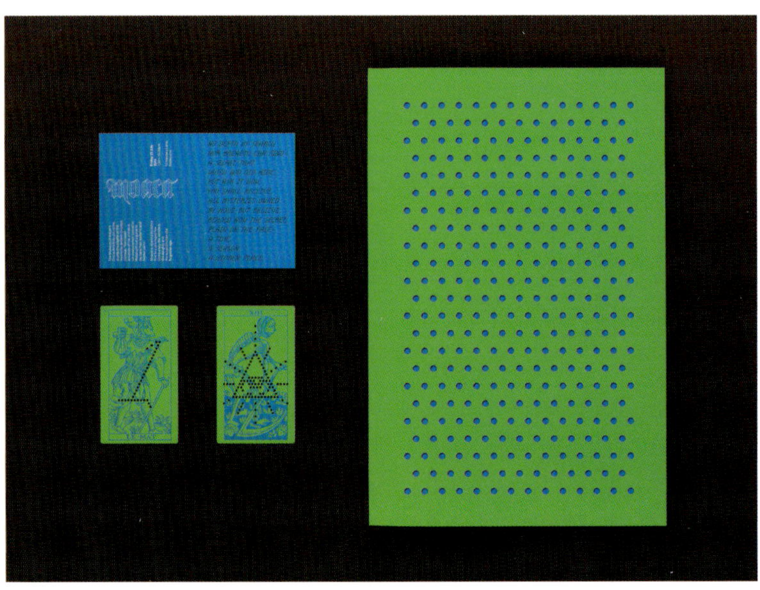

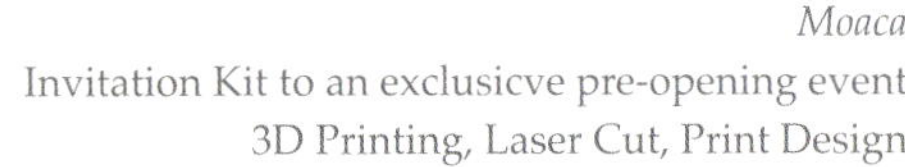

Moaca
Invitation Kit to an exclusicve pre-opening event
3D Printing, Laser Cut, Print Design

The Salty Sailor Co
Branding identity for a fish & chip shop

Monash University

STEVEN MITCHELL

SARAH MOTE

Monash University

Haz Terrarium
Reclaimed printer and scanner materials
Industrial Design

Beehaviour
Educational iPad application

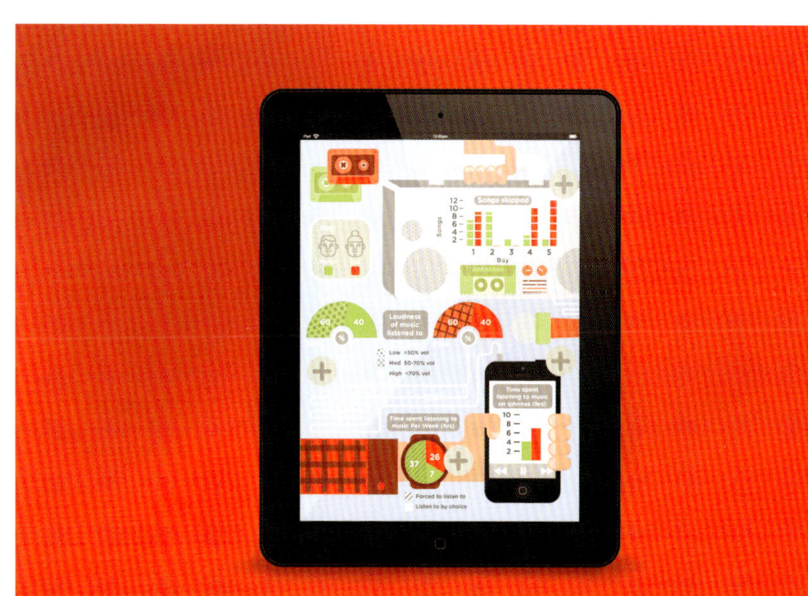

Swinburne University

NATHAN NANKERVIS

CONLAN NORMINGTON

Swinburne University

Comedy Channel Identity
Motion Graphics

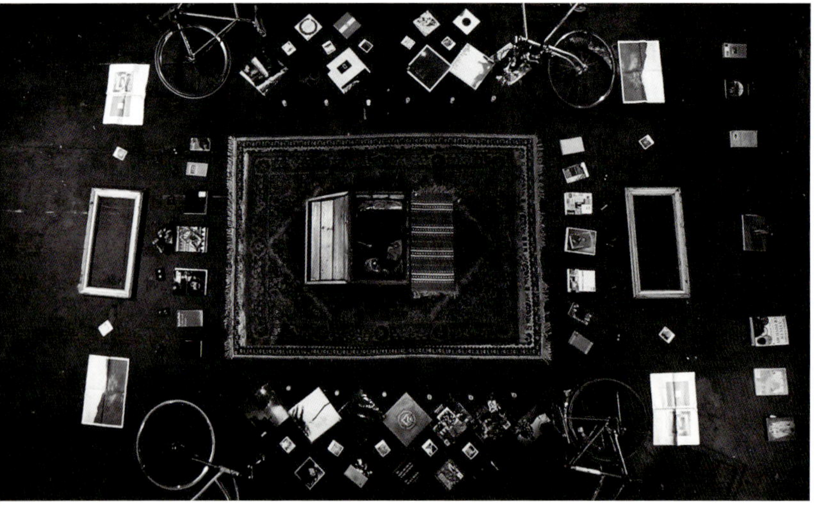

Self Portrait
An arrangement of all current posessions,
with writing and illustration
Film and Graphics

TAFE SA

TYRONE ORMSBY

NGAIO PARR

Queensland College of Art

Song Companion Set
Typesetting reflecting the tone, rhythm and intent of chosen song

Horse Product Design Festival
Campaign Identity

Shillington College

TE KANI PRICE

CLAIRE QUIRK

RMIT University

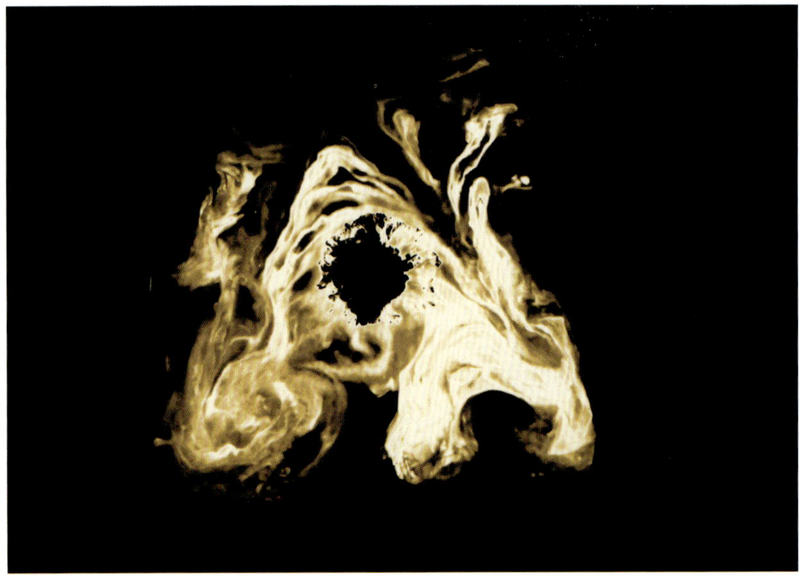

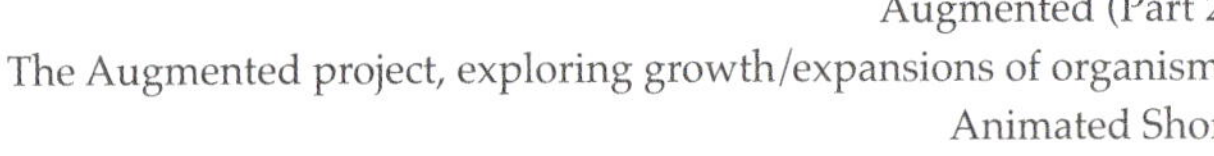

Augmented (Part 2)
The Augmented project, exploring growth/expansions of organisms
Animated Short

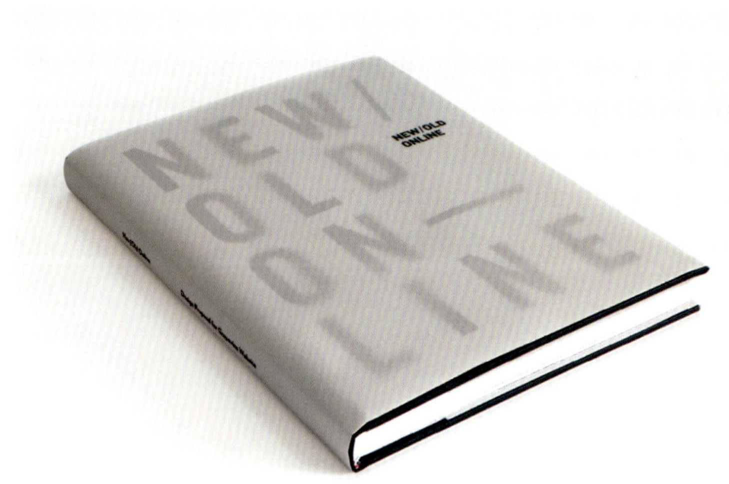

New/Old Online
Proposal for the Grapevine, a website aimed at alleviating isolation amongst the elderly
Publication Design

Swinburne University

ANDREW ROBERTSON

SIMONE RODRIGUES

Australian Academy of Design

GeoBlock Clay Necklace
Coloured Polymer Clay

Assymetry Fashion Conference
Poster Design

Shillington College

SANA SALMAN

MELANIE SCHONFELD

University of Canberra

Spacial Resonance
Piano Museum for the School of Music
Architecture

Miniature Character Sculptures
Industrial Design

Monash University

TAHL SWIECA

MITCHELL THOMPSON

TAFE SA

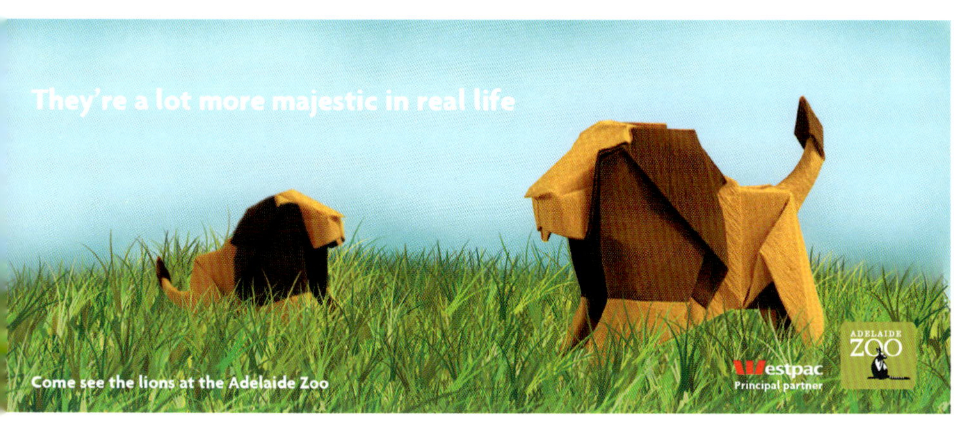

Adelaide Zoo Newspaper Ad
Advertising Campaign

The Orange Project
Raising Awareness for Palm Oil and Orangutans
Interactive Infographic iPad application

Swinburne University

STELLA TSAKIRIS

STELLA TSAKIRIS

Swinburne University

Hello Sam
Branding & Typography

Nexus Fringe Guide
Duotone program for a season of diverse shows

University of South Australia

DAN VAUGHAN

University of South Australia

Pop Up
Adelaide's vibrant 'pop up' festival culture
Poster Design

The Royal Tenenbaums
Expressive typography used to convey the meaning, tone and aesthetic of the Wes Anderson film.
A3 Poster

Swinburne University

SPEAKERS

SPEAKERS

CORDULA ALESSANDRI

— Austria —

CORDULA ALESSANDRI

One of Austria's most talented and awarded designers and educators, Cordula Alessandri is well known for her distinctive work in packaging, corporate identity, wine and food labels, annual reports, publications and websites.

Cordula attended the University of Applied Arts in Vienna, where she majored in graphic design, winning the award for top student. She then trained for three years with her typography mentor Professor Joey Badian, before, at the age of 24, becoming the first woman in Austria to be appointed an art director at DDB Needham Worldwide, Vienna.

In 1987, Cordula founded her own studio, alessandridesign, which has since enjoyed enduring success and won numerous awards, including the Austria National Award for Book Design, the European Design Award, ADC of Austria awards, ADC of Europe awards, ADC New York awards, TDC Tokyo awards, Best Calendar Awards, Golden Label Awards, Red Dot Awards and a Golden Pixel Gold Award.

Cordula has taught communication design at the University of Arts in Saarbrücken, Germany, and is regularly invited to serve on design competition juries and give lectures and presentations, in which she focuses on concepts such as 'sense and sensuality in design'.

Cordula became a member of Alliance Graphique Internationale in 2003.

Chateau de Roquefort
Corporate & Label Design Series, 2008
© **alessandridesign**

Gruber Winery
Corporate & Label Design Series, 2013

Domaine La Louviere
Corporate & Label design Series, 2013
© **alessandridesign**

Intercell
Annual Report for a
Biotech Company, 2007

The Madeira Collection
Label Design series, 2011–2013

PHILIPPE APELOIG

— France —

PHILIPPE APELOIG

From graphic designer for the Musée d'Orsay to artistic director of the Louvre Museum, Philippe Apeloig has forged a distinguished career as one of the foremost designers in the cultural arena, noted for his posters and typography.

After studying design in Paris, Philippe took up an internship with Wim Crouwel's studio in Amsterdam and at 23 was appointed graphic designer for Musée d'Orsay, where he implemented the visual identity and designed the emblematic poster for its first exhibition, 'Chicago, birth of a city'.

Awarded an arts grant, Philippe worked in Los Angeles with April Greiman, a leading New Wave designer. Returning to France, he created his own studio and also taught typography.

He moved his studio to New York and was appointed a teacher at the Cooper Union School of Art and curator of the Herb Lubalin Study Center of Design and Typography.

Back in Paris, Philippe became a design consultant to the Louvre, then artistic director for five years until 2008.

Subsequent work has included posters for exhibitions and cultural events and visual identities and logos for prestigious institutions, publishing houses and luxury brands. He is currently working on the signage for the Louvre Abu Dhabi, which opens in 2016.

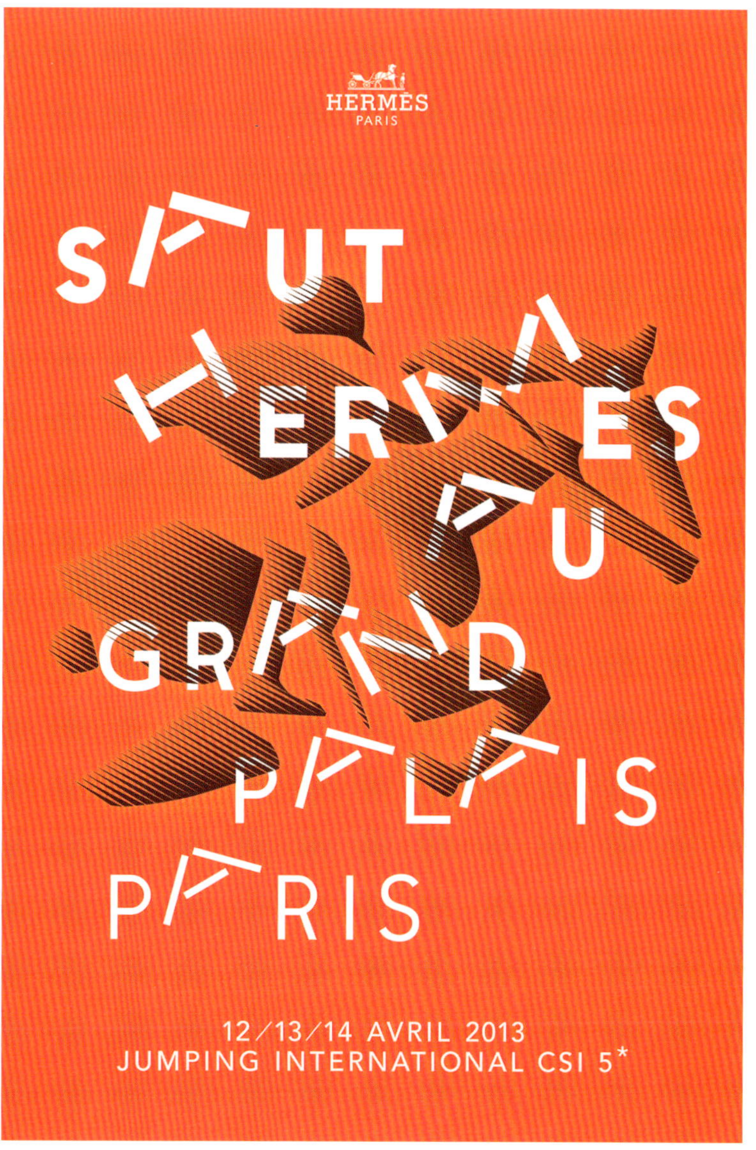

Saut Hermès
Hermès equestrian show at the Grand Palais, Paris
© Design Philippe Apeloig, 2013

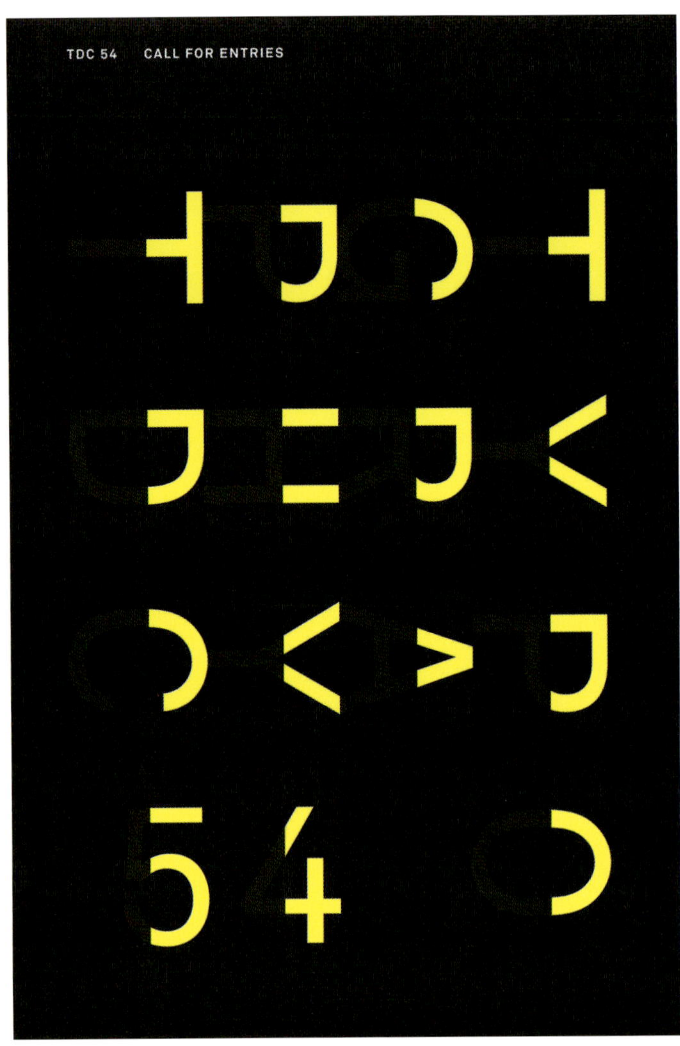

TDC 54 Call for Entries
Type Directors Club Awards
Poster Design, 2007
© Design Philippe Apeloig

Yves Saint Laurent
Retrospective Exhibition – Petit Palais, Paris
Poster Design, 2010
© Design Philippe Apeloig

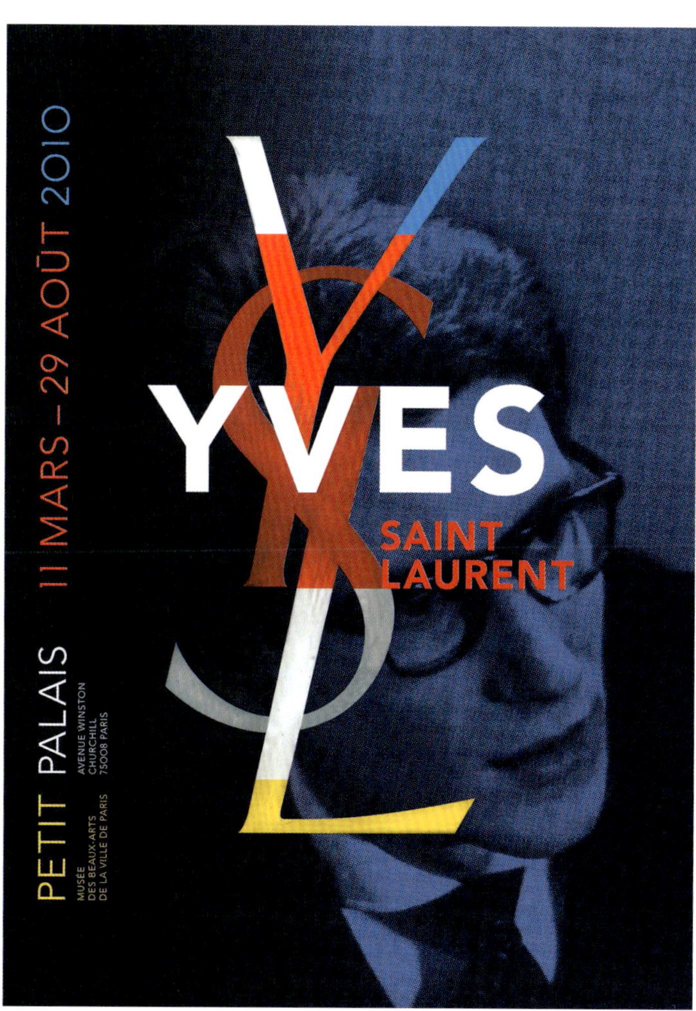

Le Havre
Competition for City
of La Havre, Poster, 2006
© Design Philippe Apeloig

bruits du monde

FÊTE DU LIVRE

18–21 OCTOBRE 2012 CITÉ DU LIVRE AIX-EN-PROVENCE

Bruits du monde
Fête du Livre, Aix-en-Provence
Poster, 2012

ANDRÉ BALDINGER

— Switzerland —

ANDRÉ BALDINGER

André Baldinger is renowned in Europe for his work as a designer, typographer and art educator.

After studying typography in Zurich and type design in Paris, André set up studio in 1995, working on commissions for cultural institutions as well as alternative projects, stage sets and three-dimensional works.

Type design has always been an integral part of André's practice and he has designed numerous typefaces, including the AB Eiffel font for the Eiffel Tower signage project.

In 2008 he established a design office in Paris with Toan Vu-Huu and their work in editorial design, artist books, posters, type design, visual identities and signage systems has since been regularly published and exhibited internationally.

Their many distinctions include a Swiss Federal Design Award (book design) and awards from the Type Directors Clubs of Tokyo and New York; International Poster Triennial, Toyama; International Biennial of Graphic Design, Brno; and Poster Triennial, Trnava.

A teacher from the earliest days of his career, André currently lectures in typography and type design at Zurich University of the Arts, EnsAD university of decorative arts in Paris, and the National Workshop for Type Design in Nancy, France. He has been a member of Alliance Graphique Internationale since 2002.

L'Ensemble
Con Moto
Flûte Annick Delorme
Violon Maxellende Doris
Alto Jérôme Eskenazi
Violoncelle Pat Griffiths
Telemann
Haydn
Mozart
Les Bayérades
Samedi 11 août 2012 à 18h00
Église Notre Dame de Bayers
Entrée 7 €, enfants: gratuit
www.amisdebayers.com

Les Bayérades
Concert Poster, 2012

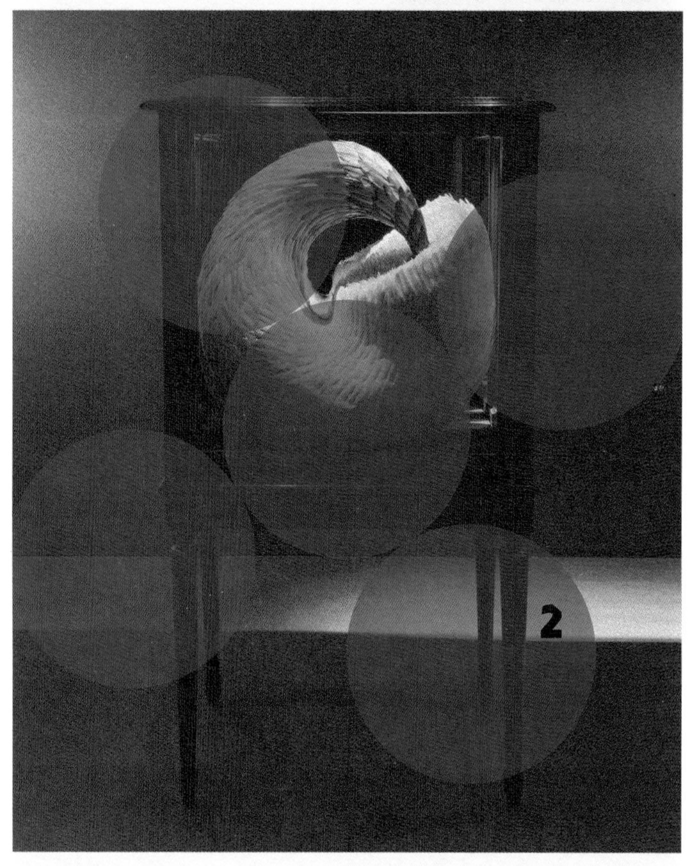

Blackbird 2
Célia Houdart Lecture Performance Poster, 2012
© André Baldinger, 2012

Atelier National de Création Typographique ANCT

ANCT

C'est en 1985 que le Ministère de la Culture a décidé de mettre en place dans les locaux de l'Imprimerie nationale, l'Atelier national de création typographique (ANCT), afin de donner un nouvel élan à la création et de relancer ce qui fut une grande tradition française. Le but de l'Atelier est de constituer un centre d'expérimentation assurant la formation artistique, scientifique et technique de spécialistes dans les domaines de la création de caractères, de la conception typographique et du design graphique. Chaque année, selon les places disponibles, l'Atelier national de création typographique propose à des étudiants et professionnels très motivés des bourses leur permettant de poursuivre leur recherche dans le domaine de la typographie, durant une ou deux années, à un niveau équivalent à un troisième cycle. La méthode pédagogique de l'ANCT incite les étudiants à se projeter dans l'avenir, pressentir les demandes des concepteurs-utilisateurs et du milieu industriel. Ainsi la recherche expérimentale peut fusionner avec les contraintes de la réalité et intégrer des données culturelles et techniques en constante mutation. L'Atelier offre aux candidats le choix d'axer leur recherche dans une discipline particulière et de développer ainsi leur profil professionnel personnel. Les directeurs de recherche encadrent les projets et guident leur réalisation par des méthodes favorisant la créativité de chacun. Des liens étroits avec l'Imprimerie nationale et de nombreux contacts avec des personnalités extérieures concrétisent le désir d'ouverture et d'échanges de l'Atelier avec le milieu professionnel.

Pour poser sa candidature:
Lettre de motivation accompagnée d'un curriculum vitæ détaillé, à faire parvenir avant le 31 mai 1993. Les candidats retenus seront convoqués par courrier pour présenter un dossier de travaux personnels en relation avec le dessin de lettre et la typographie, devant le jury de sélection. Les stages débuteront début octobre et se termineront à la fin du mois de juin de l'année suivante. Les stages peuvent être renouvelés une fois.

In 1985, the French Ministry of Culture launched the National Institute for Typographic Research, housed by the Imprimerie nationale, for the promotion of typography and type design. The Imprimerie nationale has played an essential role throughout the history of this field. The principal aim of the Institute is to encourage experimental research and training in type design, typography and graphic design, while taking full account of the scientific, technical and creative aspects of the profession. Each year, the Institute offers a one or two year grant to students or professionals who wish to pursue research in these areas. The program is situated at the level of a master's degree. The educational approach of the Institute invites students to project themselves toward the future, to keep an open ear to the demands of the creative and industrial world. Experimental research should therefore be closely linked to the constraints of economic reality, while integrating the constantly changing cultural and technical factors. The program offers students the possibility of doing research in the specialization of their choice. Close ties with the Imprimerie nationale and frequent contacts with respected designers and specialists in the field underline the openness of the Institute and its close links with the professional world outside.

To apply:
Candidates are to send a curriculum vitæ and a letter of intent before May 31th, 1993. The successful candidate is chosen by a jury on the basis of a strong portfolio and an accompanying discussion of the work. The term begins in October, 1993 and ends on June 30th, 1994. The grant may be renewed for a second year.

Pour tous renseignements, veuillez consulter le secrétariat de l'ANCT.
For further information, please contact the ANCT office.

ANCT
Imprimerie nationale
27, rue de la Convention
75732 Paris CEDEX 15
Téléphone (33-1) 45 77 84 41
Fax (33-1) 45 77 01 04

Culture

Atélier Nationale de Creation Typographique (ANCT)
Promotional Poster, 1993

Ecole Estienne
Visual Identity and signage, 2008–2010

Jaques Ripault Book
Architecture monographie, 2012

KYM BARRETT

— Australia / USA —

KYM BARRETT

Kym Barrett's skills as a costume designer have propelled her from the National Institute of Dramatic Arts in Sydney to the film sets of Hollywood.

It was at NIDA that Kym met director Baz Luhrmann, who engaged her as wardrobe assistant on his debut feature 'Strictly Ballroom' (1992) and then as costume designer on 'Romeo + Juliet' (1996).

Kym has gone on to design costumes for 'The Matrix' (1999), 'Three Kings' (1999), 'Red Planet' (2000), 'From Hell' (2001), 'The Matrix Reloaded' (2003), 'The Matrix Revolutions' (2003) 'Speed Racer' (2008), 'The Green Hornet' (2011), 'The Amazing Spiderman' (2012) and 'Cloud Atlas' (2012).

Kym has also designed for the Metropolitan Opera's 'Tempest', Cirque du Soleil's 'Totem' and recently completed principal photography on 'Jupiter Ascending' in London.

For her work on screen, Kym was nominated in 2001 by the Costume Designers Guild of America for Best Costume Award for 'The Matrix' and won the Guild's award for Best Commercial Costume Design in 2002. That year she was also nominated for a Golden Satellite Award for 'From Hell' and in 2007 was nominated for excellence in costume design for 'Eragon'. Her work on 'Cloud Atlas' earned nominations from the Critics Circle and the Costume Design Guild.

Red Planet
Costume Design, 2010

The Matrix
Costume Design, 1999

The Amazing Spiderman
Costume Design, 2012
© Sony publicity kit for public

Three Kings
Costume Design, 1999

Cloud Atlas
Costume Design, 2012

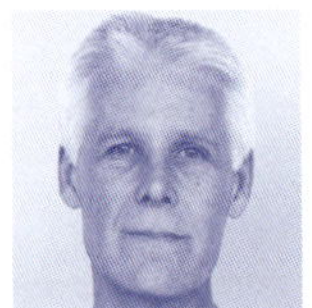

JOHN BIELENBERG

— USA / Germany —

JOHN BIELENBERG

John Bielenberg is a designer, entrepreneur and imaginative advocate for a better world. He is the founder of Project M and co-founder of Future, a company that takes inspiration and lessons from Project M.

John delights in helping people find the courage and sense of humour to bring their stories, ideas and ingenuity out into the world–the wilder and crazier, the better.

Believing that 'thinking wrong' can lead to creative success, his design philosophy is 'be bold, get out, think wrong, make stuff, bet small and move fast!'

Through Project M, John inspires and educates young designers, writers, photographers and filmmakers by proving that their work, and wrongest thinking, can have a positive impact on their communities.

In 2013, John was awarded the AIGA Gold Medal, the highest honor of the design organisation. It is one of more than 250 awards he has received throughout his career. The San Francisco Museum of Modern Art has acquired six of his design projects.

John was the recipient of the 2011 National Association of Schools of Art and Design Citation for outstanding work and overall impact in the fields of art and design as an author, educator, social activist and designer.

Presented at 'Look Upstairs' in association with RMIT University.

I AGREE TO DO SOMETHING MEANINGFUL WITH MY LIFE.

____
(your name)

____
(your email)

____
(your city)

By signing this form I agree to do something meaningful with my life. Further, I give the (blank)LAB designers permission to take photographs of me with my brand new white t-shirt and use said photographs in future materials related to the above identified subject matter. I authorize the (blank)LAB designers to use my photograph with or without my first name, my surname, or my mother's maiden name and for any lawful or unlawful purpose, including but not limited to (blank)LAB publicity, celebrity endorsements and fast food advertisements. (blank)LAB assumes no responsibility or liability for errors or inaccuracies, but we're always willing to admit when we're wrong. Information included is not legal advice. Use of any supplied materials constitutes acceptance and understanding of these disclaimers.

(blank)Lab
Project M contract, 2010

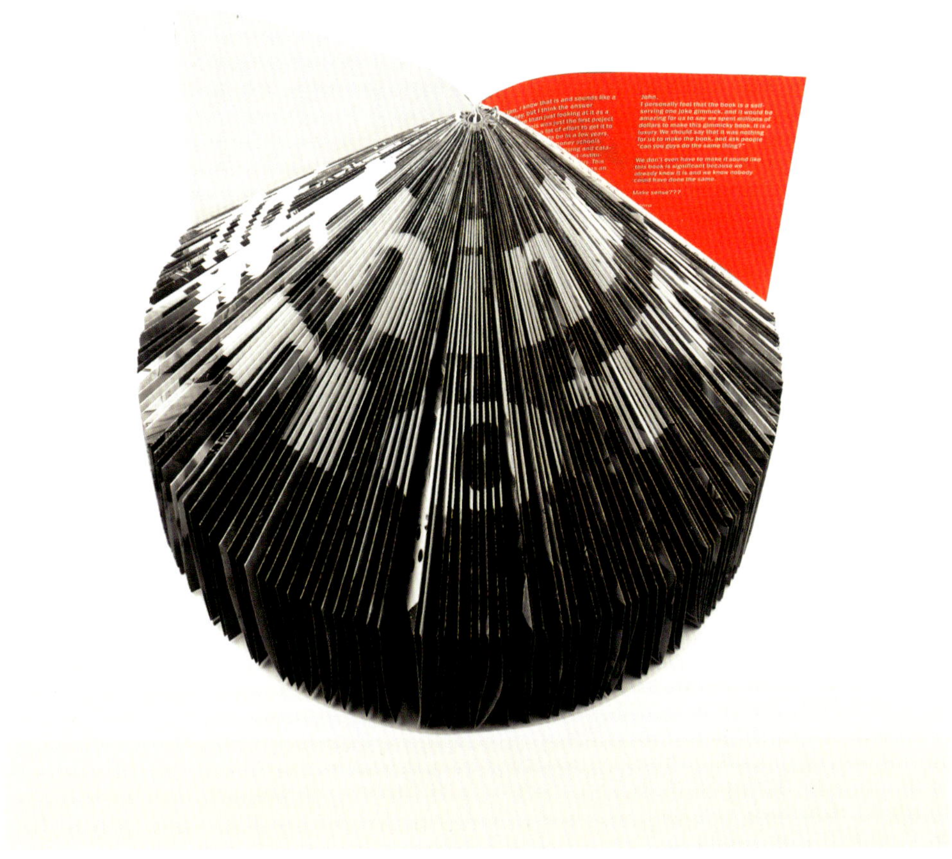

Think Wrong book
Project M book, 2003

Offenfurt/Frankenbach
Project M Frankfurt rebranding, 2011

Alabamboo
Project M bamboo bike project, 2012

Wrong Campaign
Project M campaign, 2008

PAUL BOUDENS

— Belgium —

PAUL BOUDENS

The work of Belgian graphic designer Paul Boudens is distinguished by a restless, often multi-layered and hand-finished style that has become closely identified with Antwerp fashion.

Paul doesn't like designs with a shelf life of only one day, wanting his work to be tangible and to have sensitivity. For him, design doesn't work using a computer alone and so he applies paint and other materials. While the result can be rough or sharp, somewhat broken or leaving a strange impression, it always has an effect.

After graduating in graphic design and illustration, Paul was approached by fashion guru Walter Van Beirendonck to design prints for his collection. Assignments from other leading fashion designers followed, along with work on posters and publications for the Antwerp Fashion Academy and MoMu, the fashion museum of Antwerp.

Paul also ventures into other disciplines, working for choreographer Anne Teresa De Keersmaeker's Rosas dance company and for the Brussels' opera and Kaaitheater.

He co-founded the quirky designer-led publication A Magazine and his work has been the subject of the monograph 'Paul Boudens Works Volume 1', and exhibitions at MoMu and The Wapping Project in London.

Paul became a member of Alliance Graphique Internationale in 2008.

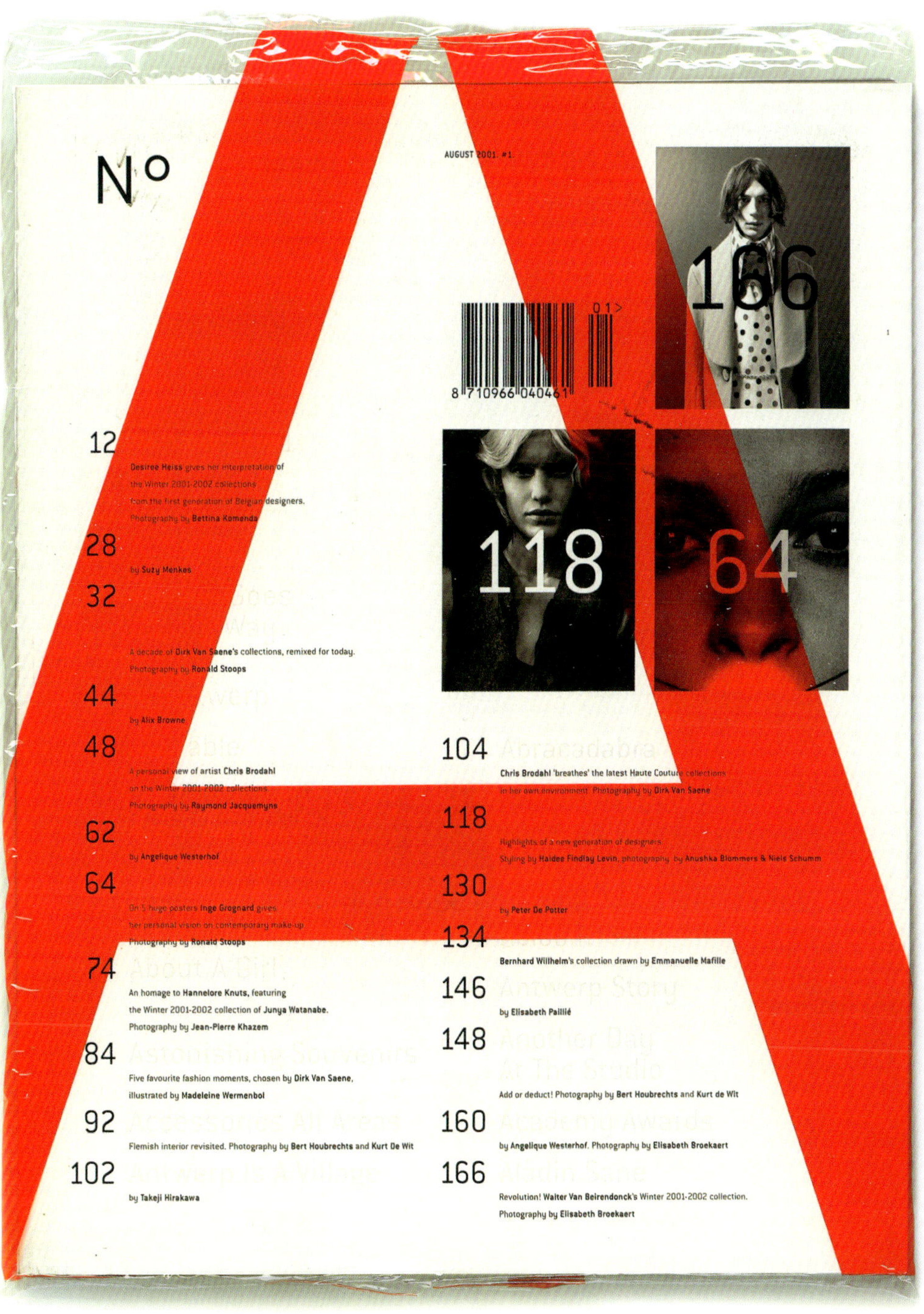

N°A Magazine

© Paul Boudens, 2001

INGE
GROGNARD
RONALD
STOOPS
WORK
PAUL
BOUDENS
INK ON
CANVAS

Paul Boudens Expo 2003

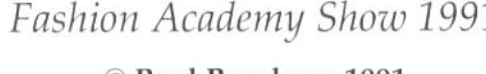

Fashion Academy Show 1991

© Paul Boudens, 1991

Yohji Yamamoto SS 2004

© Paul Boudens

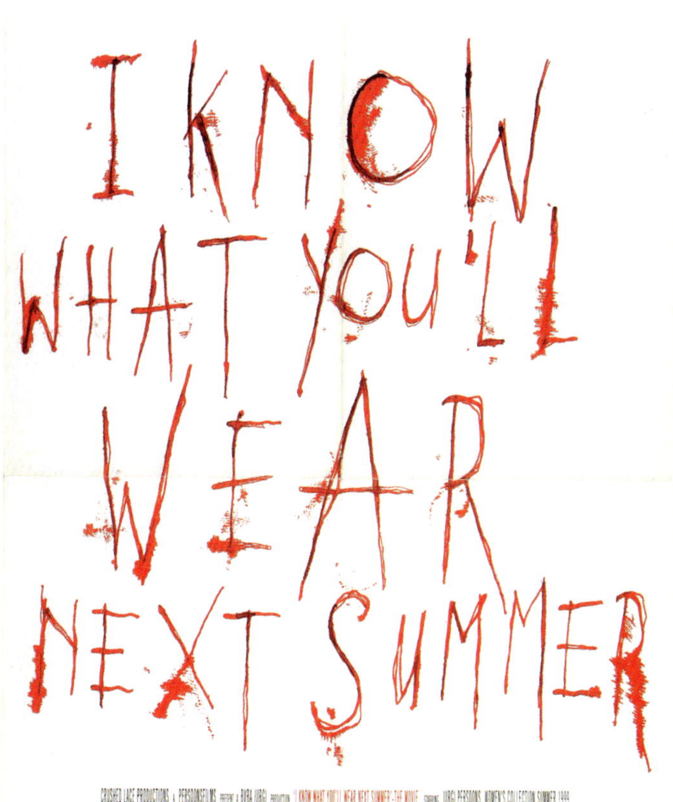

Jurgi Persoons SS1999

© Paul Boudens

WESLEY BURT

— USA —

WESLEY BURT

Wesley Burt is an outrageously talented concept artist with Massive Black in San Francisco, one of the world's biggest and most successful design studios for video games and film.

He's worked on numerous high-profile projects including the 'Fallout' franchise, all four 'Transformer' films, the 'GI Joe' movies and toys, 'inFamous 1 & 2', various 'Lord of the Rings' properties, 'League of Legends' and other projects with Microsoft, Sony, Marvel, EA, Hasbro, Warner Brothers, Capcom, Sega, Nike and Wizards of The Coast.

It all began when Wesley attended The Cleveland Institute of Art, Ohio, studying for his fine arts degree. He began exploring his interest in concept art and entertainment design, building a portfolio, participating in online communities and eventually supporting himself with freelance work.

After graduating, Wesley moved to San Francisco to join up with some friends who were creating an art out-sourcing studio for the video game industry, the first of its kind. That studio became Massive Black, where Wesley has worked for ten years now, focusing primarily on character design and illustration.

Wesley also pursues his interest in traditional arts, mainly graphite drawings and oil paintings, exhibiting at galleries in San Francisco, Los Angeles, Portland and Berlin.

Deathstroke Character Concept
Digital Painting, 2012

Fiendslayer Paladin, Magic: The Gathering
Digital Painting, 2012

D'Artagnan Advanced Version
Digital Painting, 2013

Rohirrim Camp Concept
Digital Painting, 2011

Optimus Battle Concepts
Digital, 2009

FRANCESCO CALVI

— Australia —

FRANCESCO CALVI

One of the Australia's leading lighting designers, Francesco Calvi has been involved in the entertainment lighting industry for more than 30 years, always in demand for his skills in console programming and lighting design and direction.

After working with established lighting production houses, Francesco set up his own company, Calvi Lighting Designs, in 1998. That year, he was nominated for Best Lighting Designer and two years later won the award.

Francesco's extensive list of credits includes lighting designer and director for the live TV shows 'Big Brother', 'So You Think You Can Dance', 'Australian Idol', the ARIA Awards and the Brownlow Medal.

Major events have included the official openings of Stadium Australia, the Sydney Super Dome and Fox Studios; the launches of the Toyota Camry and Lexus; and various industry awards ceremonies.

Among his concert credits are Cold Chisel's 'Light the Nitro Tour', 'Starstruck', Jose Carera and Marina Prior performances, The Great China Circus and INXS.

Fashion shows include the Australian Fashion Awards, Brisbane Fashion Week, David Jones and Myer fashion launches, Mode Fashion on Ice and Sydney Fashion Week.

Francesco has also designed the lighting for productions of the stage shows 'Aladdin' and 'Cinderella' at the State Theatre, Sydney.

The ARIA Awards
Lighting and Set Design, 2003

The X Factor
Set and Lighting Design, 2008

Nickelodeon Kids Choice Awards
Set and Lighting Design, 2011

Young Talent Time
Lighting Design, 2012

Big Brother
Set Design, 2006

KEN CARBONE

— *USA* —

KEN CARBONE

The co-founder and chief creative director of the Carbone Smolan Agency, Ken Carbone is among America's most respected graphic designers.

Under his design ethos of 'unify, simplify, amplify', Ken has created design programs for clients such as Morgan Stanley, Christie's, Tiffany & Co, Mandarin Oriental Hotel Group, Canon USA and institutions such as the Museum of Modern Art, Chicago Symphony Orchestra, Natural History Museum of Los Angeles and Louvre Museum.

Ken is the author of 'The Virtuoso: Face to Face with 40 Extraordinary Talents', celebrating human achievement in all walks of life, and co-author of 'Dialog: What Makes a Great Design Partnership', commemorating his 35-year collaboration with business partner Leslie Smolan.

He is also an accomplished guitarist.

A board member of AGI New York, Ken frequently speaks to audiences about the value of strategic design and communications in the corporate, consumer and cultural sectors. He is professor at the School of Visual Arts, New York, and a featured blogger for Fast Company, Co.Design and Huffington Post.

Ken's work has been recognised by the AIGA, Print, Graphis, Idea, Communication Arts, ID, the New York Art Directors Club, and he's a recipient of the Visionaries! Award from the Museum of Arts & Design.

In 1982
a slice of pizza
was only
75¢

AIGA/NY 30th Anniversary Exhibition
Poster Design, 2012

Musée du Louvre
Environmental Graphics
& Wayfinding, 1988
Carbone Smolan Agency © 1988

SPE Certified
Brand Identity & Design System, 2012
Carbone Smolan Agency © 2012

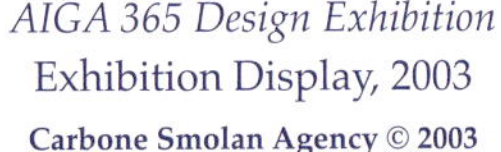

AIGA 365 Design Exhibition
Exhibition Display, 2003
Carbone Smolan Agency © 2003

Aether
Branding, 2008
Carbone Smolan Agency © 2008

RAYMOND COFFEY

— UK —

RAYMOND COFFEY

Ray Coffey is a highly accomplished artist who carved out a long and successful career in commercial design before making the switch to fine art.

In a small studio at his Brisbane home, Ray creates highly detailed portraits, full-scale figures and images of imagination, working mostly in charcoal.

His work is inspired by thoughts on humanity's need to distance itself from the animal, why time and place have more effect than perceived choice, and how our lives are shaped by random uncontrollable events.

Born in Liverpool, England, from an early age Ray immersed himself in European comic books, fascinated by the amazingly detailed art.

He spent most of his youth copying his favourite artists, hoping one day to become one himself.

At the age of 17, Ray began as a commercial artist and worked on a great number of projects for more than 25 years.

After immigrating to Australia in 2004 and becoming a citizen in 2009, he decided it was the right time to change direction and realise his long ambition of becoming a fine artist.

Ray has exhibited around Australia and has been a finalist in several national art prizes, winning three people's choice awards in 2013.

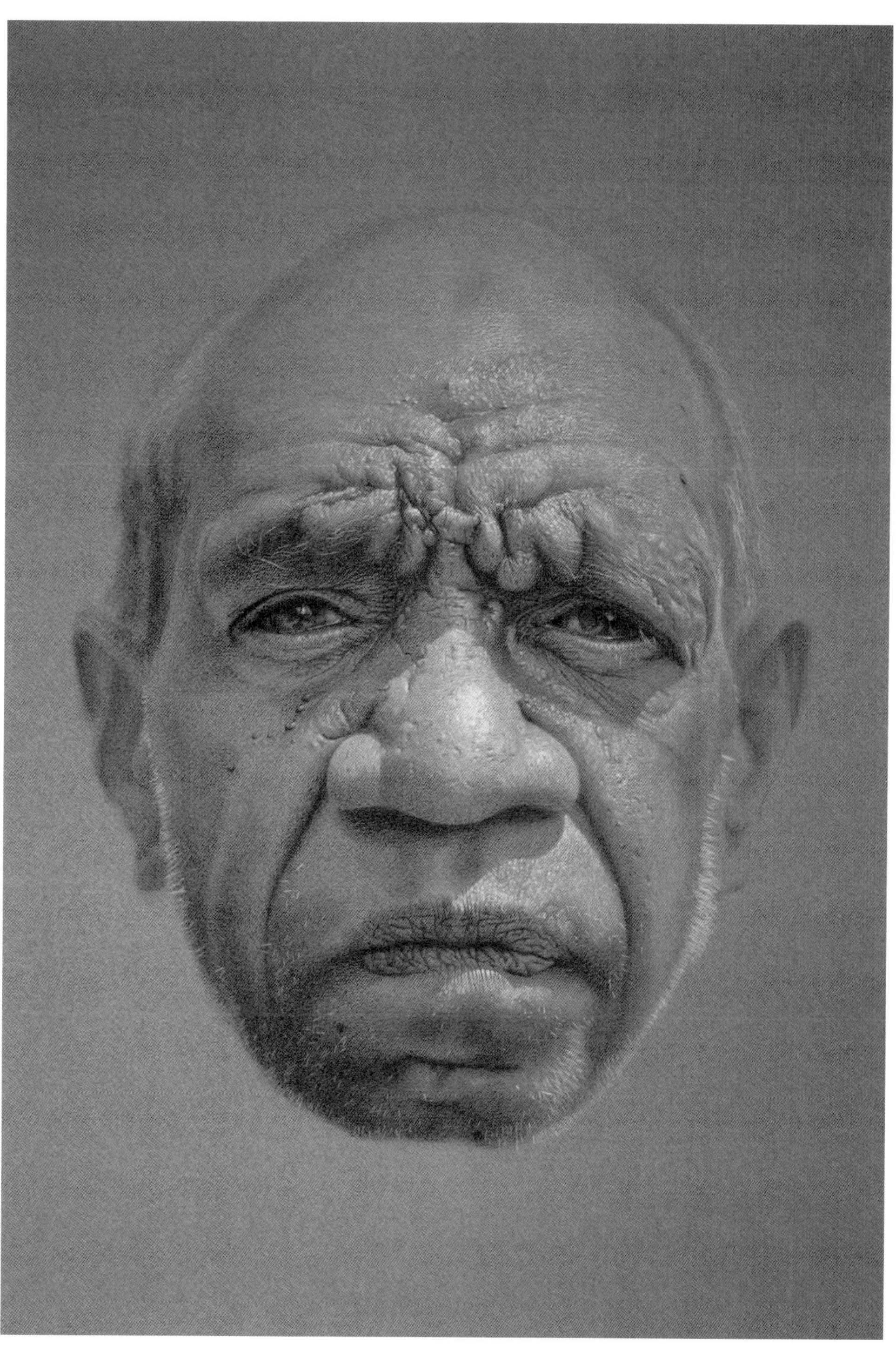

Kevin
Charcoal on Canson paper
Homeless Series, 2013

Ernie
Charcoal on Canson paper
Homeless Series, 2013

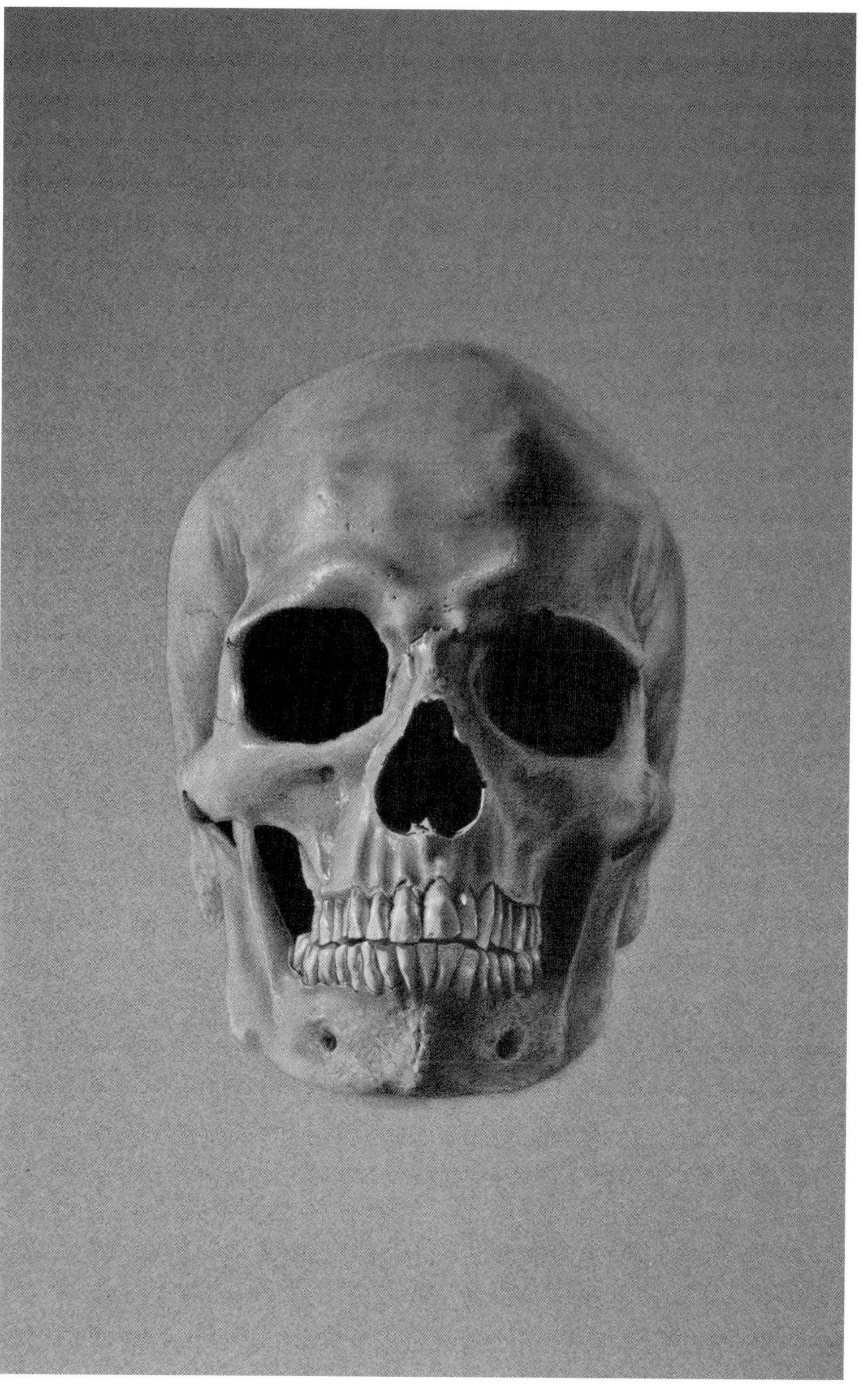

Skull
Charcoal on Canson paper
First exhibition, 2012

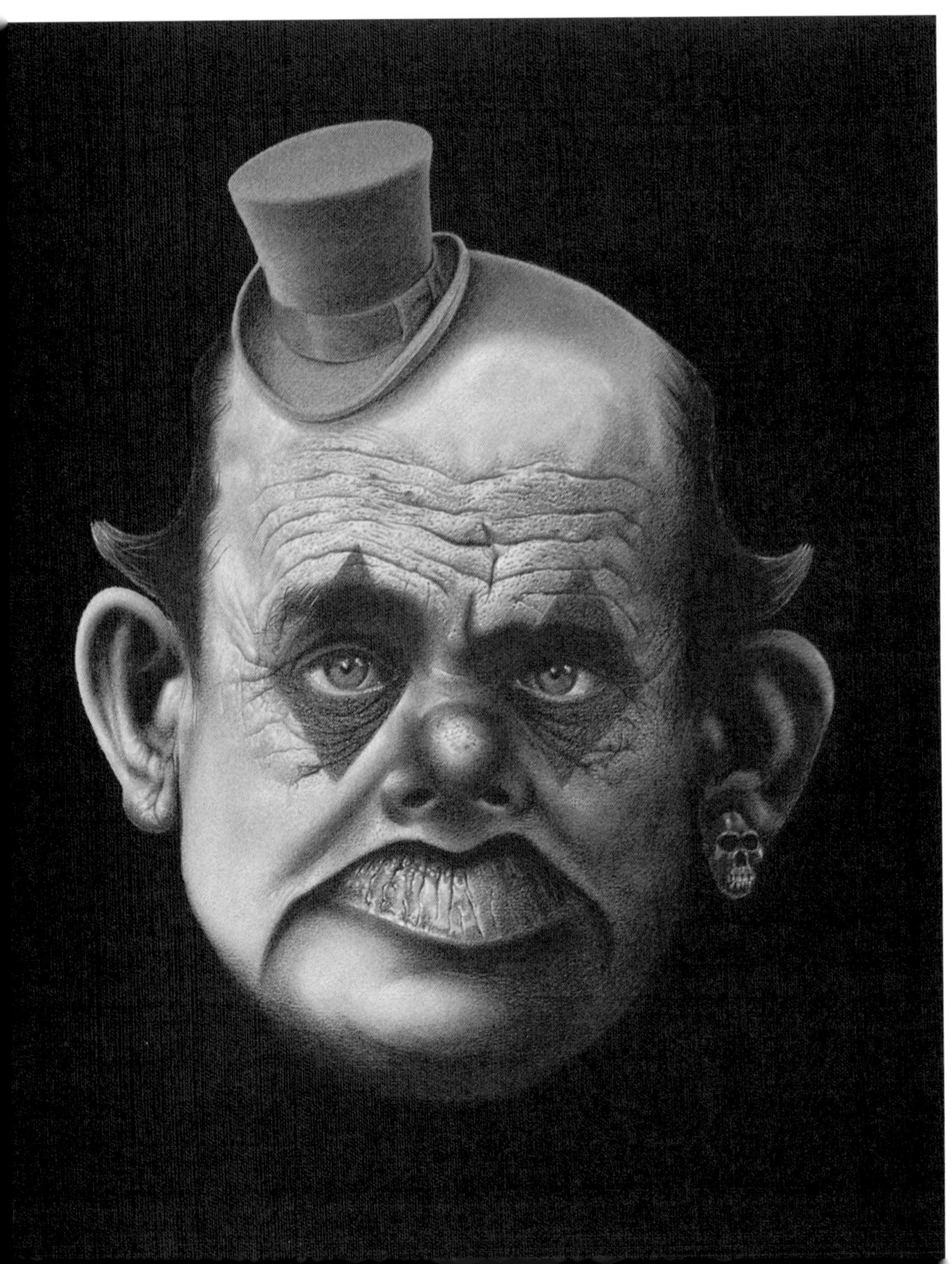

Clown
Charcoal on Canson paper
First exhibition, 2011

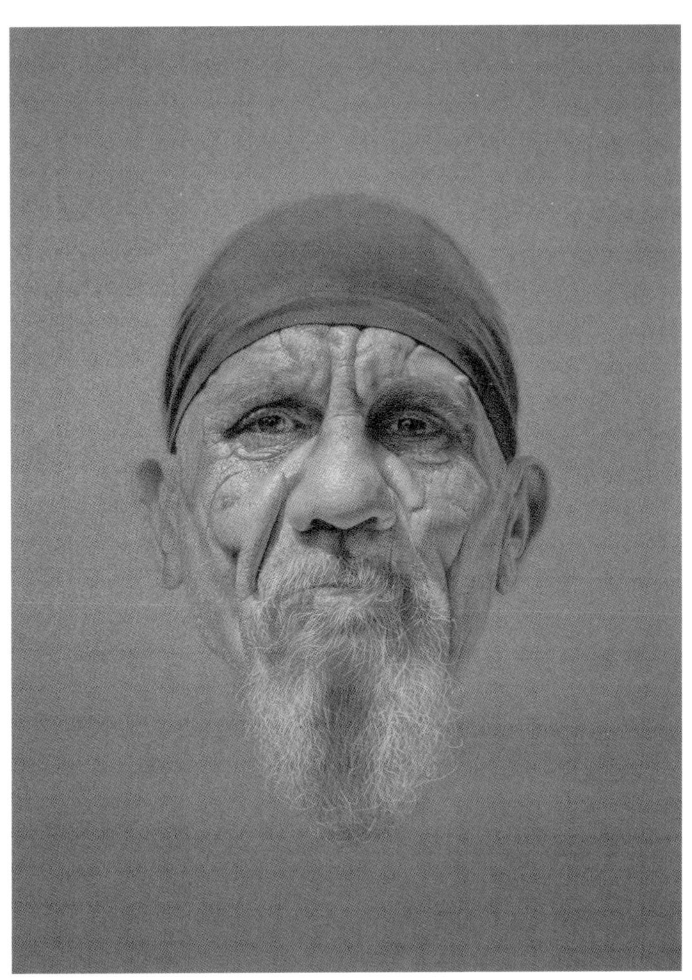

Daniel
Charcoal on Canson paper
Homeless Series, 2013

ROWENA CURLEWIS

— Australia —

ROWENA CURLEWIS

Rowena Curlewis is co-founder and managing director of The Collective Design Consultants, a specialist drinks design consultancy in Sydney.

Founded in 2002 with creative director Margaret Nolan, the company's clients range from major wine companies, such as Treasury Wine Estates, Taylors Wines and De Bortoli Wines, to boutique brands such as House of Cards, Dexter and Yabby Lake Vineyard.

Rowena splits her time between managing the company and working on client projects on a daily basis.

Her career in design began after roles in publishing, marketing and advertising in Sydney, London and Toronto. She joined design firm Landor in 1995, where Penfolds was one of the first packaging projects she managed, and the relationship has been maintained since then.

It was while working as client services director at Kirby+Nolan that Rowena met Margaret. The two worked together on various product categories but wine company projects interested them most.

Since forming The Collective, their like-minded thinking and a healthy respect for each other's abilities has resulted in a profitable and rewarding business, producing work that is both effective and award winning.

Rowena has a BA in Communications from Charles Sturt University and management qualifications from AGSM University of NSW.

Clover Hill,
Packaging, 2009
Clover Hill © The Collective 2009

Elefante
Packaging, 2010
Elefante © The Collective 2010

Squealing Pig
Packaging, 2009

this little pig went to ~~market~~ xxxxx Marlborough
this little pig stayed home
this little pig had ~~roast beef~~ xxxx xxx cool fermentation
this little pig had ~~none~~ xx minimal handling
this little pig went wee wee wee

La Bohème
Packaging, 2010
La Bohème © The Collective 2010

Este
Packaging, 2011
Este © The Collective 2011

GIUSEPPE (PINO) DEMAIO

— Australia —

GIUSEPPE (PINO) DEMAIO

Behind his flourishing beard, Giuseppe Demaio thrives on having an iron in many creative fires.

After completing degrees in marketing and design at Monash University and studying at the Fabrica design research centre in Italy, Giuseppe was publisher of the iconic Colors Magazine before being appointed editor and art director of the Belgian design publication Addict Magazine.

Following a stint as senior art director at Nike EMEA, in 2009 he founded the Melbourne-based brand communications agency Local Peoples, which works across design, film, retail and experiential design for clients such as Alpha 60, Nike, Red Bull, Australian Unity, Harvard University, Melbourne University, Vice, Adidas, L'Oreal Melbourne Fashion Festival, Levi's, Addict Magazine, Qantas and The World Health Organisation.

Giuseppe is also a co-founder of Assemble, an architecture and property development company that focuses on affordable small-footprint living and publishes Assemble Papers, an online publication covering architecture, art, design, urbanism, the environment and financial affairs.

In 2013, Giuseppe and his brother Alessandro founded NCDFREE, a global movement against non-communicable diseases (NCDs), which kill 35 million people each year, mainly in poor and marginalised communities. The group's campaign highlights young change-makers working to prevent NCDs through community action, stories and films.

Nike +Nine
Experiential design and delivery 2012
Local Peoples, © Giuseppe Demaio, 2013

Nike Laser II Campaign
Campaign art direction and design
Local Peoples, © Giuseppe Demaio, 2013

Nike India Cricket World Cup

Campaign art direction, retail design and key visual

Local Peoples, © Giuseppe Demaio, 2013

Local Peoples & Assemble Studio
Interior design, 2012
© Tanj Milbourne, 2013

Nike Tennis Players Lounge
Experiential design and delivery, 2012
Local Peoples, © Giuseppe Demaio, 2013

AGNELLO DIAS

— India —

AGNELLO DIAS

Agnello Dias ranks among the most influential people in Indian advertising. His credits include being listed by Fast Company magazine in the world's 100 most Creative People in Business, ranking in Campaign's Global Power List of the top media personalities in the world, and being named India's Communicator of the Decade.

After starting with a local Mumbai agency, Agnello went on to lead Leo Burnett India to its first Global Agency of the year award and was voted NDTV's Creative Director of the Year in 2006.

In 2008, as Chief Creative Officer of JWT India, he made history by winning India's first Cannes Lion Grand Prix and the first Lion in the Titanium-Integrated category.

In 2009, Agnello founded Taproot India, which soon ranked among the world's top 20 independent agencies. It became part of Dentsu in 2012 and that year was crowned Creative Agency of the Year at the Asia-Pacific Adfest.

In 2013 Taproot was once again India's top agency at Cannes and rated among the top ten agencies in the world.

Agnello's work features in all the top award books including The One Show, The London International Advertising Awards, The Clios, Cannes, D&AD and The New York Festivals.

Gully Gully Mein Ganesha
The Times of India, 2013
© **Taproot**

Knife Sharpener, Born Glamorous
Bombay Times, 2012
© **Taproot**

MARUTI SUZUKI *presents*

an initiative by THE TIMES OF INDIA

THE 9TH LETTER.

It sits there amongst the group. Waiting.

No trumpets, no fanfare, nothing.
But simmering, quietly. Awaiting its turn.

For when the time is right, it can raise its head, put up its hand and turn into a war cry that could change the course of history.

Never before, has so much human belief been loaded into one single letter as this, the ninth one.

I.

Sure, it's just a stroke. But it can also be a word, a statement, an anthem, a stab of defiance, a ray of hope and the fuel of belief.

When it stands before any word, that same word can suddenly turn hope into conviction, anger into purpose and cynics into converts.

I can. I must. I am.

Today our nation stagnates. Under the dark shadows of a billion fingers pointing at one another, shouting about what should be done, how it should be done and who should do it.

We don't need any more finger-pointers. We have enough. We just need a few who will put up their hand and say, I will, I believe.

I believe that, in my own small way, I can lead a bit of the change I wish to see. That bit will be my change and I will own it.

It's time the real India stood up. It's time I stood up.

I am the I in India.

I LEAD INDIA
I WILL BE THE CHANGE

Maruti Suzuki and The Times of India, two of India's most significant change leaders join hands to launch a powerful nationwide initiative that will empower citizens to push for solid, measurable change in their cities and towns. The I Lead India campaign will kick off with the Youth Brigade across 26 Indian cities with key projects that will impact the day to day life in each of those neighbourhoods. Join the movement for change at www.ileadindia.com, facebook.com/ILeadIndia2013 and twitter.com/ILeadIndia2013.

The 9th Letter, The Times of India
Winner at Cannes Lions International Festival of Creativity, 2013

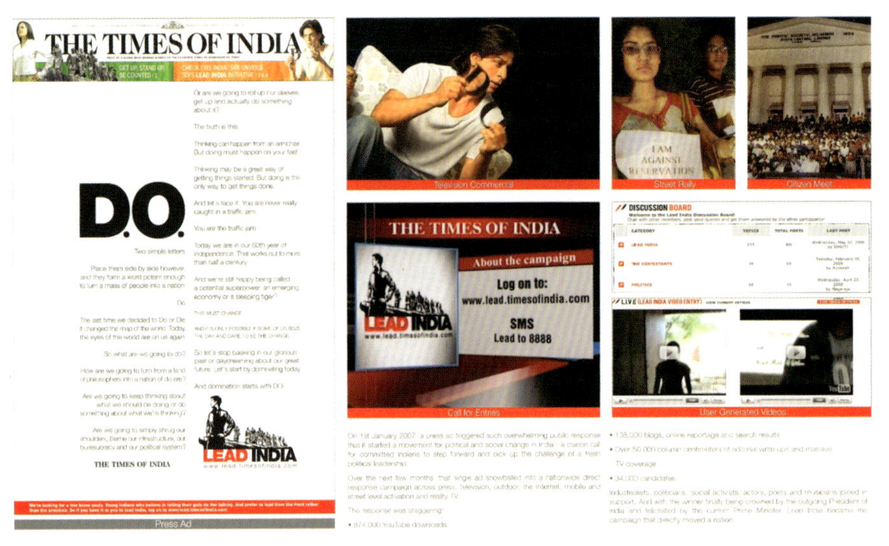

The Times India

Winner Cannes Lions International Festival of Creativity, 2013

Bandwala, Born Glamorous
Bombay Times, 2012

MARK DOUGLASS

— Australia —

MARK DOUGLASS

Mark Douglass is a master glassmaker, artist and designer who works on large-scale commissions as well as producing his own range of lighting and interior products.

His distinctively robust vases, bowls and sculptures go beyond the simply decorative and make ambitious artistic statements through the use of themes and imagery from botanical, figurative and architectural motifs.

As the principal of It Inc in Melbourne, Mark has created works for clients in a wide range of sectors including residential, retail, hospitality and hotel accommodation.

He has been responsible for the design of many projects in Australia and most recently in Macau and mainland China where he's been commissioned to design a range of feature glass installations for Crown Casino Macau, Galaxy Casino Macau, MGM Grand Casino Macau, Grand Park Hyatt Beijing, Crowne Plaza Guangzhou, Westin Hotel Xiamen and Sheraton Qiandao Lake Resort.

Mark has also exhibited successfully both in Australia and internationally, and his work can be found in many private collections.

In 2012 Mark was awarded a Churchill Trust Fellowship in recognition of his impressive body of work as a master glass artist and the contribution he has made to the Australian glass art industry over more than two decades.

Metropolis Vase
Gould Exhibition, 2009
MDD © Mark Douglass, 2009

Installations
Gould Exhibtion, 2011
MDD © Mark Douglass, 2011

3 vases
Gould Exhibition, 2006
MDD © Mark Douglass, 2006

Loreal Light
Loral HQ, 2007
MDD © Mark Douglass, 2007

Spacement Light
Spacement Gallery, 2006
MDD © Mark Douglass, 2006

DICK FRIZZELL

— New Zealand —

DICK FRIZZELL

Hawke's Bay artist Dick Frizzell often slips through the nets of traditional critical and curatorial definition, with the success of his artistic career due in part to the dramatic diversions he has made between different art styles and genres.

Before moving into fine arts, Dick worked in advertising as an animator, commercial artist and illustrator, and has no qualms about blurring the categories between his commercial work and art. His paintings are often a pastiche of images drawing on modern art and graphic design.

His work has always been characterised by an endlessly inventive range of subject matter and styles: faux-naive New Zealand landscapes, figurative still lifes, comic book characters and witty parodies of modernist abstraction.

His taste is conveniently broad and he has a penchant for fondly remembered and well-worn clichés, with his work portraying a sense of exuberance, ironic humour and baby-boomer nostalgia.

An anti-traditionalist, Dick often makes a deliberate effort to mix up the categories of high and low art, poking fun at the intellectualisation of 'high art' and the existential angst of much New Zealand painting in the art culture of his youth.

Although primarily a painter, Dick also produces works on paper, including lithographs and screen prints.

Sambuca Galliano Blu
Limited edition silkscreen print
430 × 300mm, 1996

Mickey to Tiki
Limited Edition Litho
550 × 770 mm, 1997

Often Licked Never Beaten
Enamel on Board
1000 × 1000 mm, 1981

Sambuca Galliano Verde
Limited edition silkscreen print
430 × 300mm, 1996

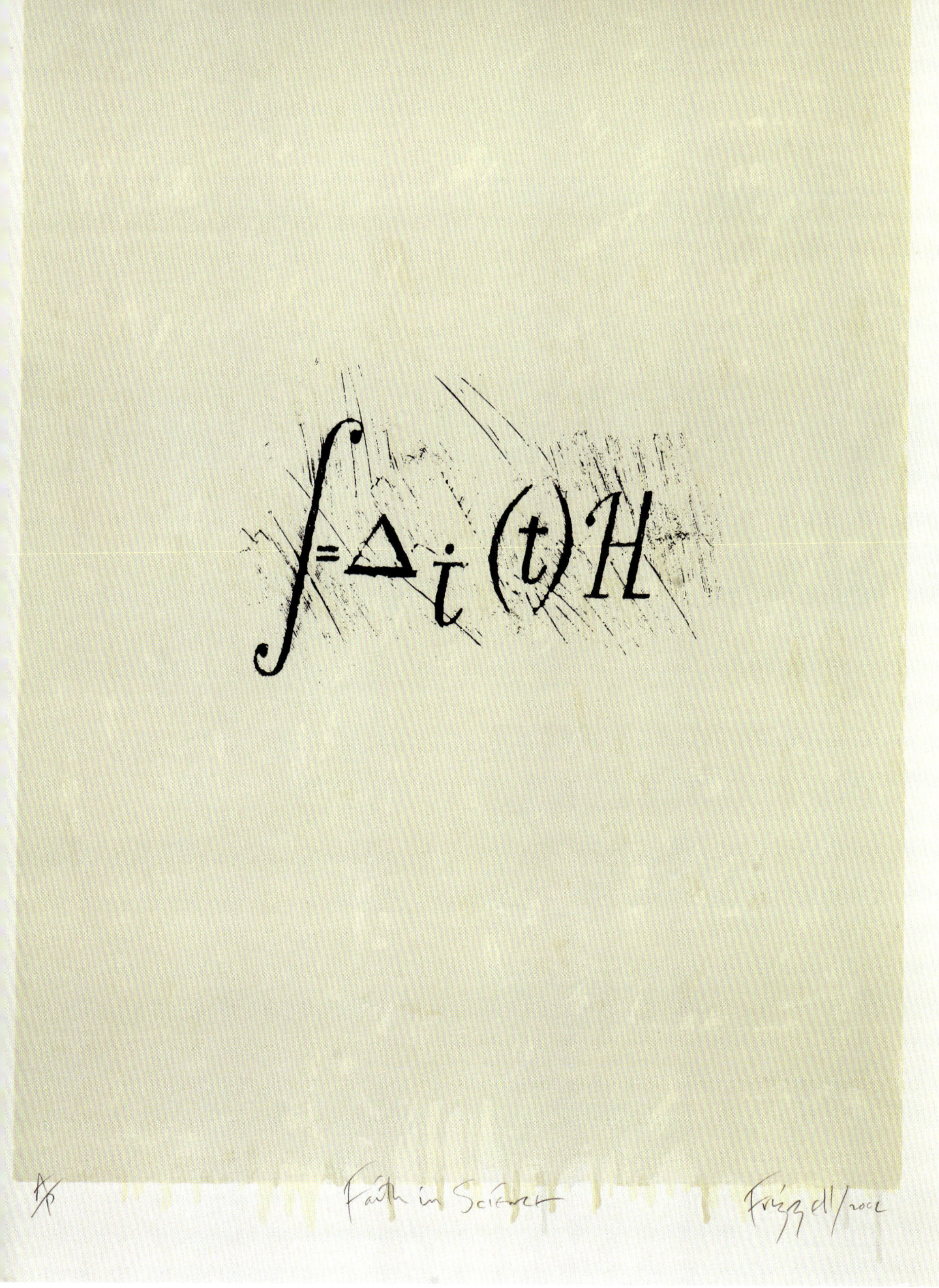

Faith in Science
Silkscreen print,
700 x 500 mm, 2002

SEAN GODSELL

— Australia —

SEAN GODSELL

One of Australia's most inventive architects, Sean Godsell is attracting international attention for his strong minimalist spaces and surfaces, intelligent use of light and innovative application of materials.

Trained at the University of Melbourne, Sean formed Godsell Associates in 1994.

He initially gained attention for his distinctive residential architecture, which ranges from single-family dwellings to 'compassionate infrastructure' projects that provide refuge for displaced persons.

More recently he has won accolades for his work on high-profile buildings such as the RMIT Design Hub in Melbourne's CBD, which won the 2013 Victorian Architecture Medal and the William Wardell Award.

His work has been published in leading architectural journals and is featured in the Phaidon Atlas of Contemporary Architecture. The influential design magazine Wallpaper has listed him as one of ten people destined to 'change the way we live'.

Sean's many other awards include the Victorian Premier's Design Award, the RAIA Robin Boyd Award, the Cappochin residential architecture award (Italy) and the AIA Record Houses Award for Excellence (USA).

Sean has lectured across Australia and in the USA, UK, China, Japan, India, Finland, France and New Zealand and in July 2013 was visiting professor at IUAV, the renowned university of architecture in Venice.

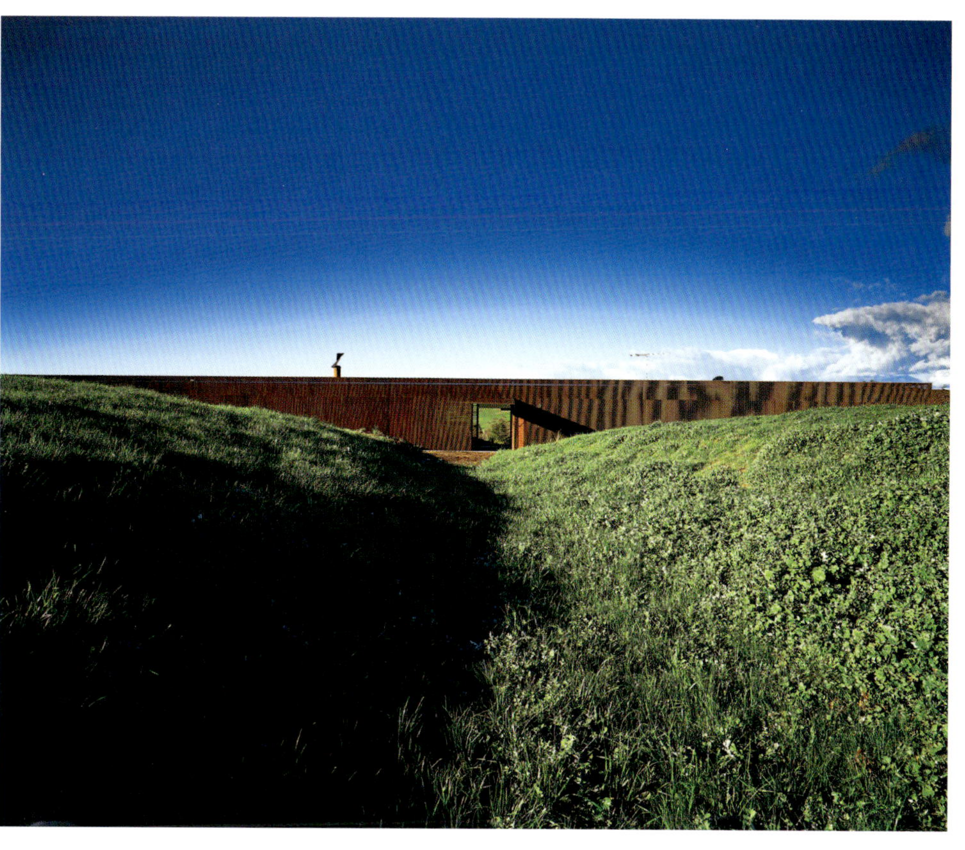

Glenburn House
Sean Godsell Architects
Photograph Earl Carter

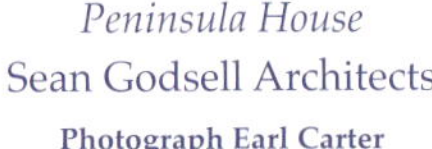

Peninsula House

Sean Godsell Architects

Photograph Earl Carter

St Andrews Beach House
Sean Godsell Architects
Photograph Earl Carter

Carter Tucker House
Sean Godsell Architects
Photograph Earl Carter

Future Shack
Sean Godsell Architects
Photograph Earl Carter

SANDRA HILL

— Australia —

SANDRA HILL

A proud Noongar woman from south-west Western Australia, artist Sandra Hill is well known for her profound paintings, prints and sculptures, which reflect her Aboriginality, spirituality and personal identity.

In 1958, aged seven, Sandra was taken from the care of her mother and, with her three siblings, placed in an orphanage for 'assimilation'. Fostered out to a white family, she stayed with them until her marriage at age 17. It was not until 1985 that Sandra was finally reunited with her biological parents.

Inspired to research her family, she set out on a journey of discovery, both in relation to her true identity and cultural heritage; her traditional clans are Balladong and Wilmen on her mother's side and Wardandi and Minang on her father's side.

Sandra's art tells of her experiences. To her it is a visual essay of the suffering and losses she and her people have suffered in the recent past; however, more importantly, she sees it as a celebration of survival, revival and, finally, a triumph of the Indigenous spirit.

Through her works, which have been exhibited widely and are held in major collections, Sandra is always endeavouring to diminish the gap between Indigenous and non-Indigenous Australians.

Home Maker #4
Oil on Linen
910 × 670 mm, 2010
© Image courtesy Indigenart – Mossenson Galleries and the Artist

Home Maker #6 – Surf's Up
Oil on Linen
760 × 910 mm, 2012
© Image courtesy Indigenart – Mossenson Galleries and the Artist

Man Maid
Oil on Linen
500 × 600 mm, 2012

Evening Star
Oil on Plywood, 1330 × 930 mm, 2012

Home-Maker #8 – The Flip-Side

Oil on Linen, 910 x 760 mm, 2012

JASON HUTCHINSON

— Australia —

JASON HUTCHINSON

A professional creative thinker, designer and problem-solver for more than 20 years, Jason Hutchinson has an unsatisfied burning desire to create, build and make things better. He has designed and implemented award-winning digital projects for some of Australia's largest organisations.

Since his appointment as the national creative director of Deloitte Digital in 2010, Jason has more than doubled the size of the creative team and helped the company establish a global reputation as a digital and creative leader.

Deloitte Digital is now around 200-strong across the nation and last year Jason became their first-ever creative partner anywhere in the world.

His extensive experience in delivering results across both traditional web and mobile has paid massive dividends, reflected in the tremendous growth of the Deloitte Digital business, and their clients' business too.

Jason's primary role these days is to ensure the highest possible creative standards on behalf of clients, partners and staff. Ultimately, however, he's still a designer at heart, rolling up his sleeves and working with some of the bright creative minds that make up his team at Deloitte Digital.

ANZ Compare Me
Digital Design, 2013

ING Australia
Mobile App, 2013

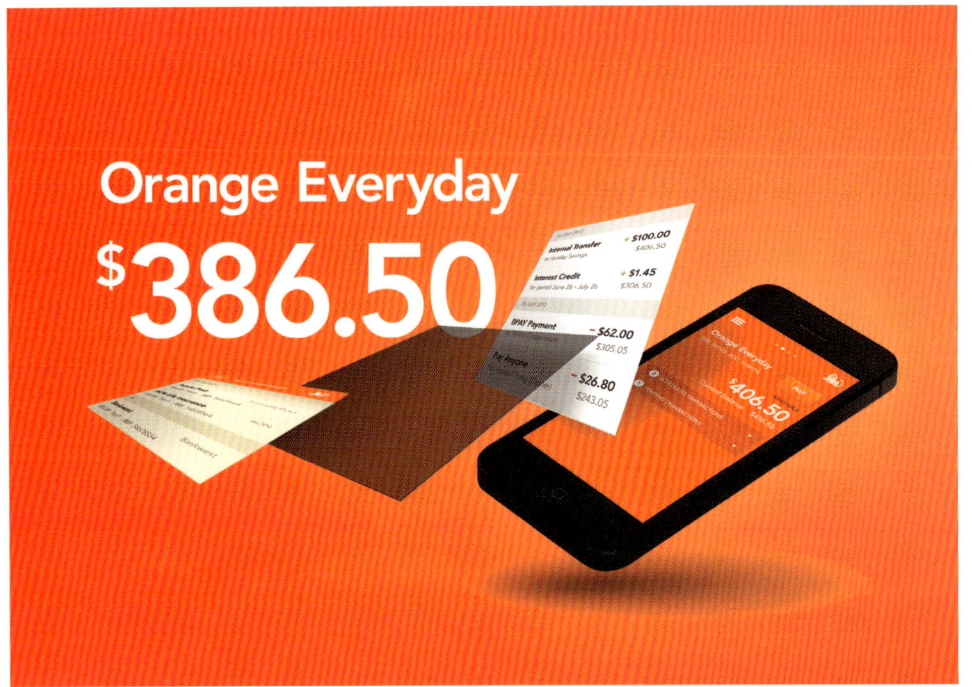

CPA
Digital Design, 2013

Australia Post
Digital Design, 2013

TimeSaver
Mobile App, 2012

ANUPAMA KUNDOO

— India —

ANUPAMA KUNDOO

Anupama Kundoo is a global architect advocating a 'whole world' approach to housing practices in order to reduce the environmental impact of building technologies.

Born in Pune, India, and currently teaching at the University of Queensland, her work focuses on the brick-by-brick detail of how structures are built, proposing architectural solutions that provide local socio-economic benefits through a holistic and contextual approach to sustainability.

This can be seen in her 'Volontariat Homes for Homeless Children' in Pondicherry, India, which uses the 'firedmud house' approach. Large mud structures are built and fired on site, eliminating the need for cement in brick masonry and achieving permanent houses using local skills and materials.

Anupama has worked and lectured around the world, including Berlin, London and New York. Her projects and writings have been featured in newspapers, journals and books such as the Phaidon World Atlas of Contemporary Architecture and AD Architectural Design London, and she co-edited Sustainable Building Design Manual Volumes 1 and 2 for the Catalan Energy Institute.

A runner-up in the 2013 ArcVision International Prize for Women and Architecture, Anupama was commended by the jury for 'her dedication when approaching the problem of affordability of construction and sustainability in all aspects'.

Wall House
12th Architecture Biennale at Venice
2012
© Andreas Deffner

Pierre Tran
Single family residence, 1991
© Andreas Deffner

Urban Eco Community
Collective housing prototype, 2003

Wall House
12th Architecture Biennale at Venice
Architecture, 2012
© **Andreas Deffner**

Wall House
12th Architecture Biennale, Venice
Architecture, 2012
©Andreas Deffner

BJÖRN KUSOFFSKY

— Sweden —

BJÖRN KUSOFFSKY

Co-founder and creative director of one of Europe's most influential multidisciplinary studios, Björn Kusoffsky espouses a design philosophy based on the fundamentals of simplicity, clarity, openness and innovation.

His work ranges from title sequences, artbooks, aircraft livery and advanced packaging projects to logos and graphics, cosmetic fragrance and wine packaging, retail environments, brand repositioning and corporate identity programs.

Since opening its doors in 1998, Björn's studio, Stockholm Design Lab, has attracted clients from Sweden and beyond, including SAS Scandinavian Airlines, IKEA, Moderna Museet, Ustra Stadtbahn (Germany), Hyundaicard (Korea), Askul (Japan) and the 53rd International Art Biennial Venice (Italy).

A member of Alliance Graphique Internationale since 2000, Björn is represented in the design collection of the National Museum of Art, Stockholm. His work has been exhibited in Tokyo, Berlin, Moscow, London, New York, Mexico, Helsinki, Köln and been featured in numerous magazines such as Wallpaper, The Wall Street Journal, Elle, GQ, Creative Review, Print and Esquire, and he has taught and lectured widely.

Björn's work has been recognised with numerous accolades, including Gold Cannes Lions and British D&AD, Red Dot Design and Swedish Advertising Association awards. He has also received the special distinction of an award for Excellent Swedish Design.

Velux D&A, Issue 15
Cover Design, 2011

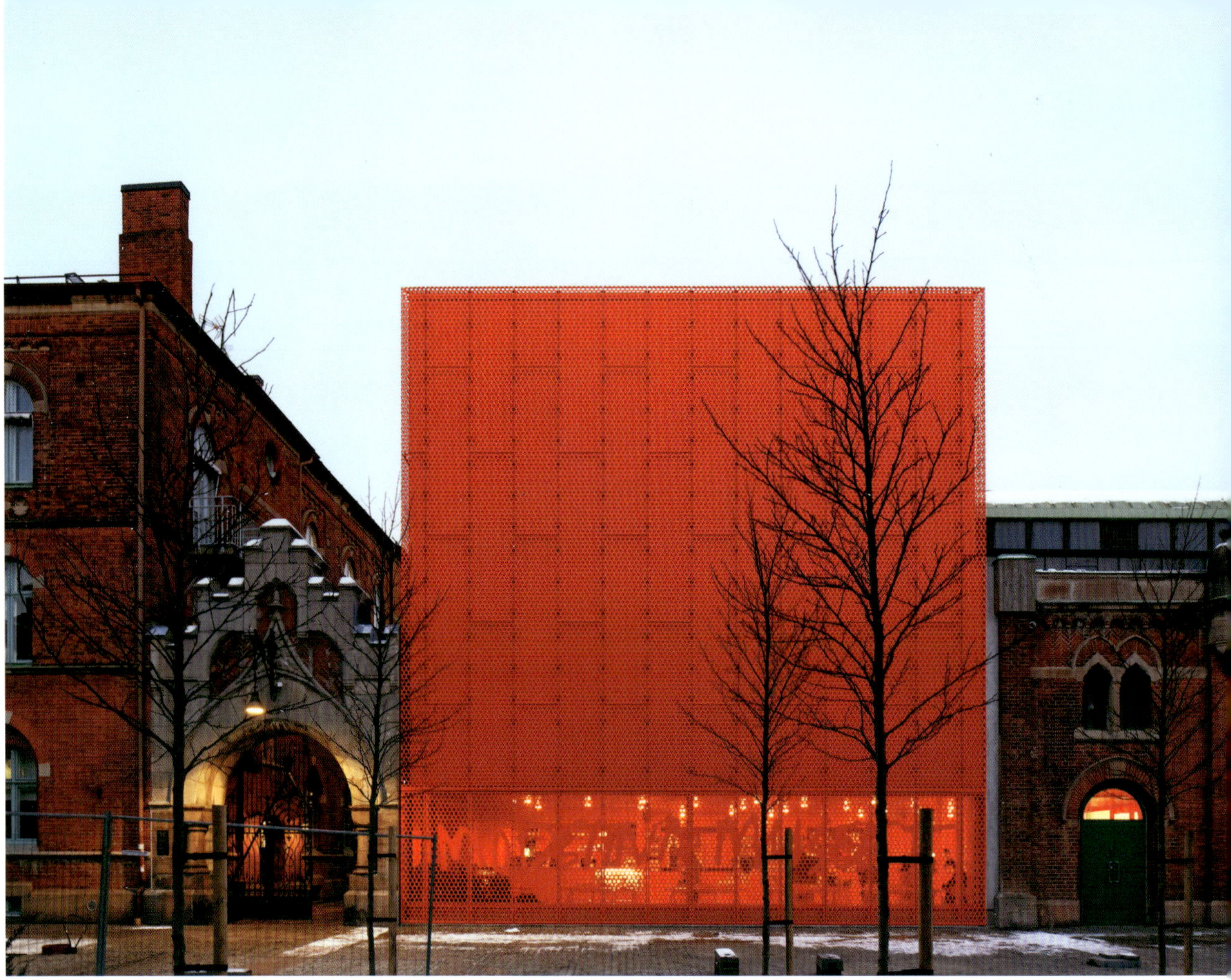

The Moderna Museet in Malmö
Exterior Facade Design, 2010

IKEA FOOD 'Skarpsill'
Packaging design, 2010

Venice Biennale
Catalogue covers design, 2009

SAS Airplane
Corporate identity, 2000

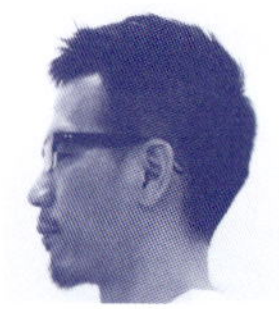

KEN-TSAI LEE

— Taiwan —

KEN-TSAI LEE

Ken-Tsai Lee has earned an international reputation as a designer, educator and curator.

As well as running his studio in Taipei, he is an assistant professor at the National Taiwan University of Science and Technology, the visual director of Taiwan Designers' Week and regional representative of the New York Art Directors Club and New York Type Directors Club.

Mentored by the Japanese design master Shigeo Fukuda, Lee established his studio in 1996. His work has since been recognised with the Taiwan National Design Award and numerous others from the leading design organisations and publications, including Design for Asia, D&AD, New York Type Directors Club, New York One Show, Tokyo Type Directors Club, Hong Kong Designers Association, Red Dot Design, Communication Arts and Graphis.

As well as participating in many design exhibitions worldwide, Lee curated the 70/80 Taiwan Designers Exhibition in China in 2008, was co-curator of the 'Post-Contemporary International Poster Retrospective' for the Beijing world design congress 2009 and leader of Taipei's bid to host the 2011 World Design Congress.

Since 2008 Lee has been touring the annual exhibition ADC Young Guns Taiwan, dedicated to identifying and honouring the best young creative talent under 30.

Chinese Characters Art Festival
Poster, 2011

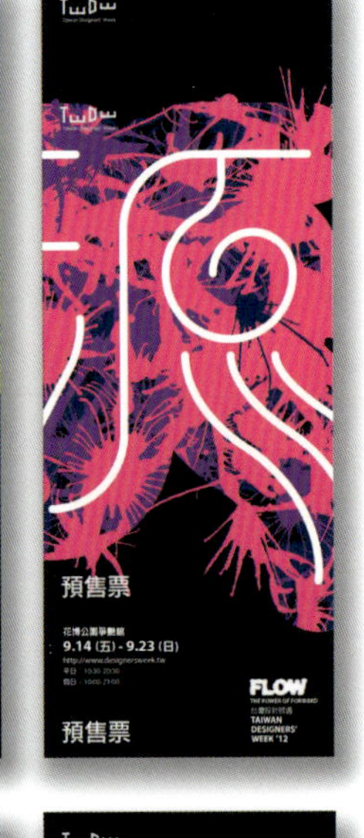

Taiwan designers' week
Branding 2012

Type Directors Club exhibition in Taiwan
Branding, 2013

Taiwan designers' week
Branding, 2013

Fonso Paper
Poster, 2007

ALEX LEHOURS

— Australia —

ALEX LEHOURS

Alex Lehours is a Sydney-based artist, illustrator, muralist and designer whose work can best be described as an eccentric explosion of chaos, humour, colour and absolute randomness.

He has worked on numerous projects, both internationally and domestically, including commissions for The Black Keys, Stolichnaya Vodka, Fuel TV, Facebook, Mad Mex, Very Nearly Almost Magazine, Westfield, Stupid Krap, Desktop Magazine and Dephect Clothing.

Alex uses inks, pens, paints, watercolours and aerosols in his work, and has declared red as his favourite colour, because it's 'bold and daring'. That gives an inkling into how his mind and art work together to create a cataclysmic visual 'boom!'

Another insight comes from exploring his bookshelves, where you'll find titles like 'The Disposable Skateboard Bible', 'The Art Of Modern Rock', 'Russian Prisoner Tattoos' and 'The Great American Pin Up'.

It's all there in one of his recent print works, 'Weird, Disgusting Behaviour', a chaotic luchador-inspired design expressing his childhood fascination with those bizarre wrestling programs on TV.

Alex has been involved in many exhibitions and live painting events at galleries, venues and events including the National Gallery of Victoria, Studio, Without Walls Volume 3, King of Nothing's Tomorrow's Nostalgia, Damp Space and Insert Coin.

The Black Keys, Gig Poster
The Black Keys Australian Tour, 2012
Alex Lehours for Beyond The Pale

Powderfinger, Vulture Street
Digital Artwork
Stupid Krap and Desktop Magazine, 2013
Alex Lehours for Stupid Krap & Desktop Magazine

In My Lifetime
Aerosol & Acrylic on Canvas
All About The Benjamin's Exhibition
New Zealand, 2013
Alex Lehours, © Alex Lehours 2012

The Renegades
Mural, The Renegades Café & Wine Bar, 2013
Alex Lehours for The Renegades, © The Renegades

Weird, Disgusting Behaviour
Digital Giclee Print, Stupid Krap, 2013
Alex Lehours for Stupid Krap, © Alex Lehours

LUKE LUCAS

— Australia —

LUKE LUCAS

Luke Lucas is a Melburnian with a highly successful self-made career in art direction, illustration, design and typography spanning two decades.

In the late 1990s Luke co-created Fourinarow, an in-line skating publication that was distributed worldwide. With two other partners he then started Lifelounge, simultaneously a creative agency, online creative culture portal and glossy print magazine.

It was through Lifelounge that Luke began to experiment with conceptual illustrative typography, custom lettering and type design, and it wasn't long before he was attracting briefs for illustrative type from agencies, publishers and brands across the globe.

His regular clients include Nike, Target USA, Esquire, The New York Times and The Washington Post, and he has received awards from D&AD, MADC and AWARD.

In 2011, as a new father, Luke made the decision to leave Lifelounge (his other baby) to spend more time with his family and pursue a full-time freelance career focusing on the work he's most passionate about: typography.

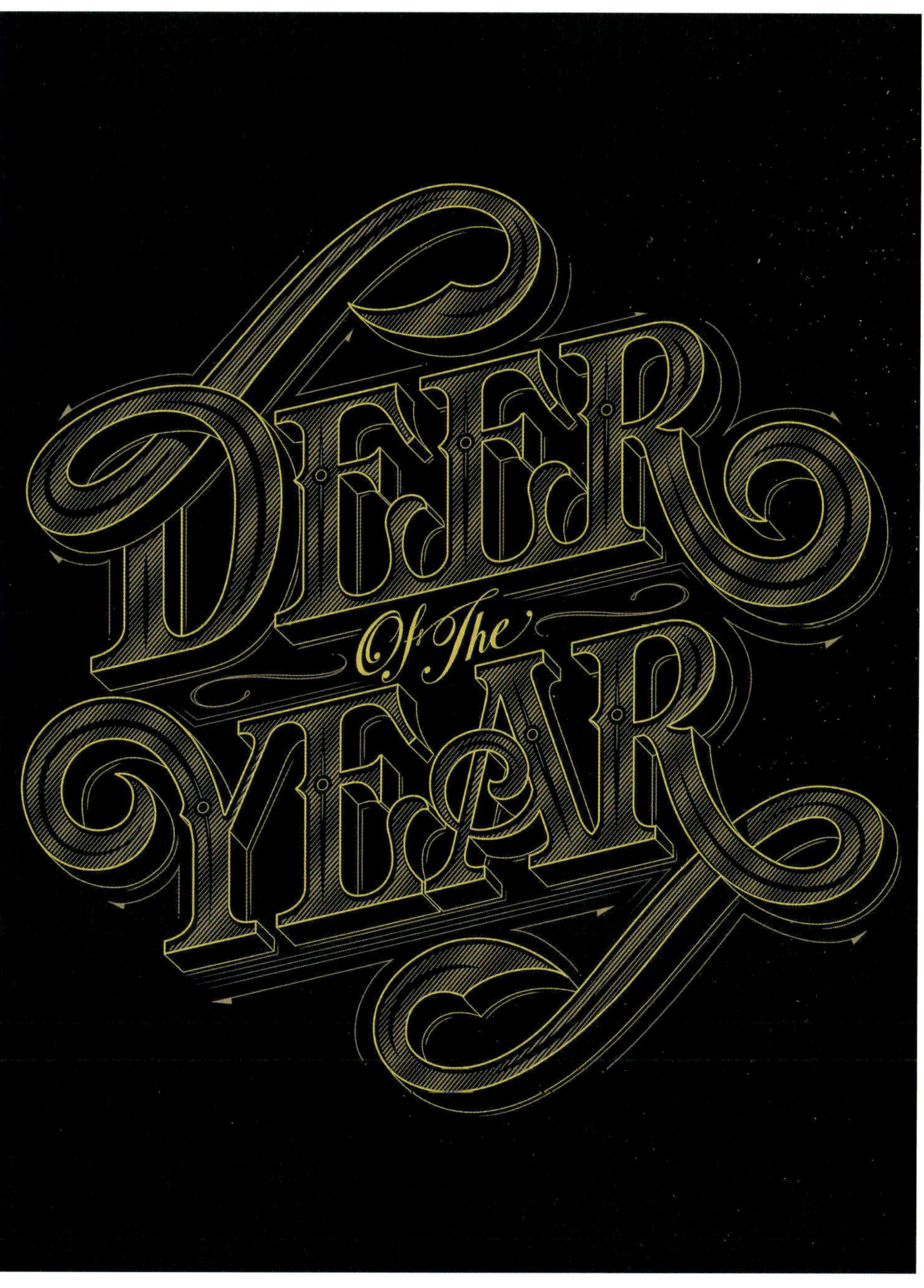

Deer of the Year
Feature lettering, Outdoor Life (US)
Magazine, 2013

The Washington Post – Q1
Business Section Cover Illustration for
The Washington Post, 2012

Hype Today Gone Tomorrow
Perspex Type
A Type Of Show exhibition
Sydney, 2011

Nike Free
Letter concept for Nike Free model
worldwide product release, 2013

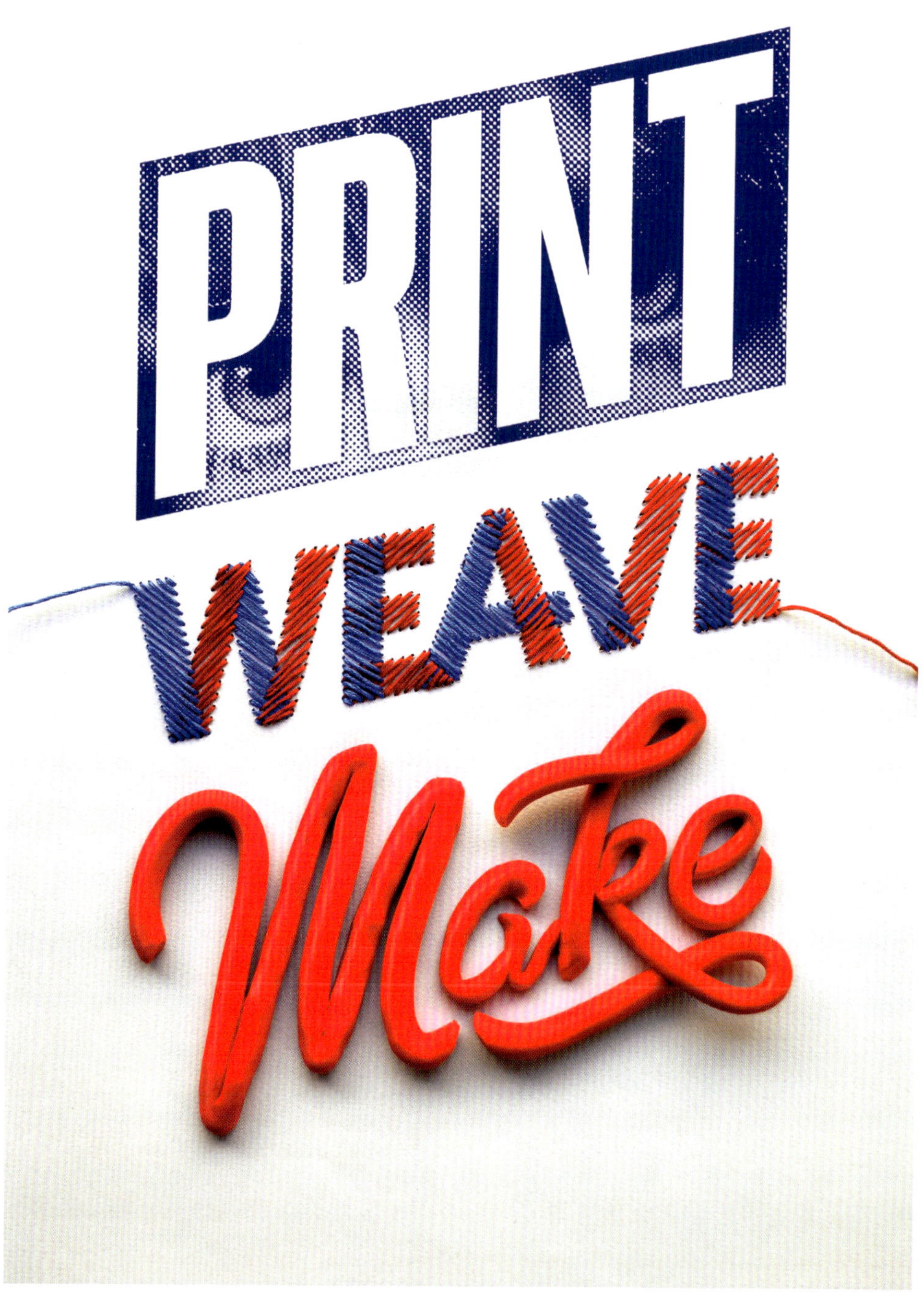

Print Weave Make ID
ID and treatment, 2012

ALEJANDRO MAGALLANES

— Mexico —

ALEJANDRO MAGALLANES

Based in Mexico City, designer Alejandro Magallanes has built an international reputation for his posters, distinctive for their reinterpretations of popular Mexican imagery, use of mixed media and visual impact.

Alejandro plays with images and words but prefers not to believe in the adage that an image is worth a thousand words, since 'a thousand words combined can create six million images, more or less'.

In his posters, illustrations and photographs, handwritten excerpts and printed fonts, caricatures and silhouettes, drawings and visual references, flat colours and shades all make an appearance.

His composition tends to place the figure in the centre of the design, facing directly at the spectator and creating a forceful presence.

Alejandro works mainly for social and cultural media and has drawn, painted, built and designed not only posters but books, animations, collages, letters and images.

He is a founding member of several activist poster groups whose work promotes peace, justice and women's rights, and has written nine children's books and a recent collection of poems.

Alejandro has been a member of Alliance Graphique Internationale since 2004. Three monographs of his work as a graphic designer and poster designer have been published in China, Spain and Germany.

Alicia 16 años
Alicia (independent concert forum)
16th anniversary, Poster, 2012

Almadía
Editorial image system, 2005–2013

Libro libro
Book, 2012

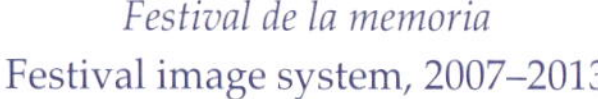

Festival de la memoria
Festival image system, 2007–2013

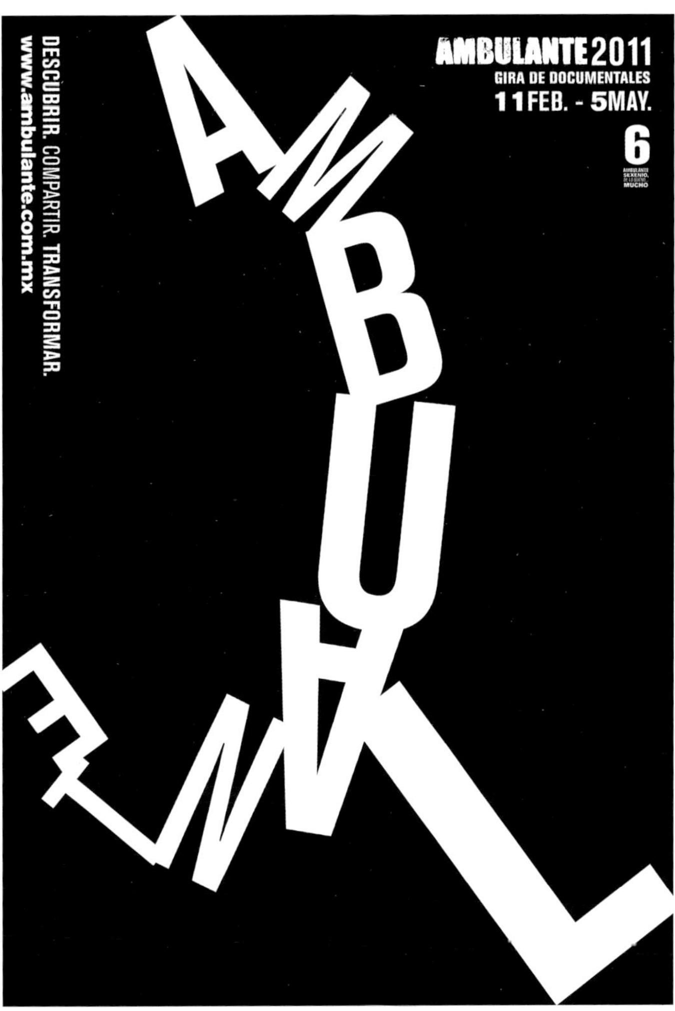

Ambulante, Gira de documentales
Ambulante documentary film festival
Poster + image system, 2011

SAED MESHKI

— Iran —

SAED MESHKI

Saed Meshki is a noted Iranian graphic designer dedicated to the process of printmaking and the design of book covers and posters. His work is distinguished by intriguing illustrations and exquisite calligraphy.

A member of Alliance Graphique Internationale, Saed is a board member of the Iranian Graphic Designers Society and is on the editorial board of the design magazine 'Neshan'.

In 2001 he co-founded the 5th Color Group to create a link between graphic design in Iran and the rest of the world and has since organised several exhibitions at home and abroad.

Saed's numerous awards include first prize for cover design at the 7th Biennial of Iranian Graphic Design (2001), the Pearl of Czech Design prize (2002), first prize at the First Biennial of Cover Design, Tehran (2003), and the Icograda Excellence Award at the 19th international poster Biennial Warsaw (2004).

He was a member of the selection committee of the 7th Iranian Graphic Design Biennial and a jury member of the first Iranian Self-Promotional Posters Biennial, the 5th Exhibition of Children's Books Illustrators and the 9th Tehran International Poster Biennial.

Saed studied graphic design at the Faculty of Fine Arts at Tehran University and is now teaching there.

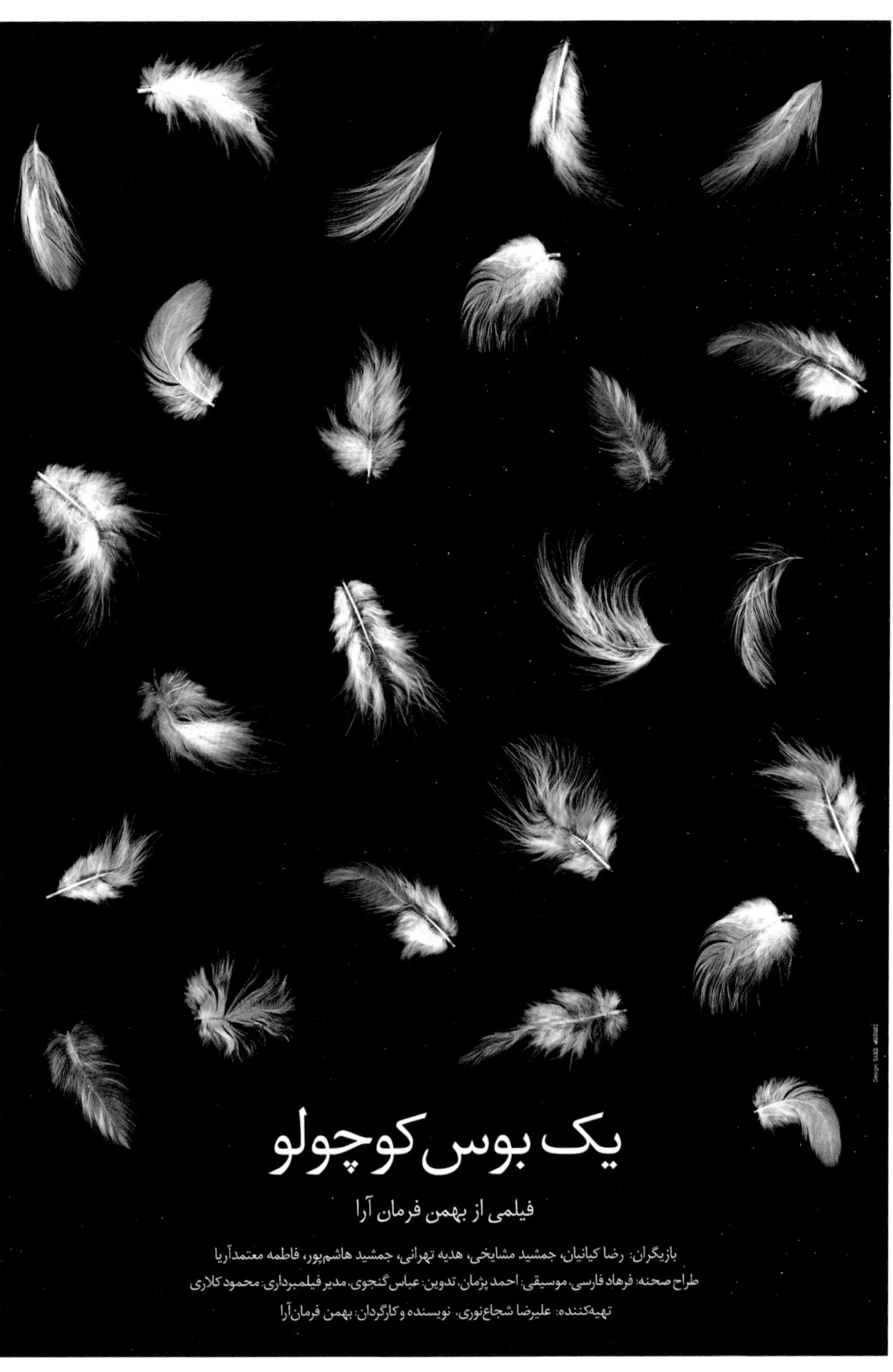

A Little Kiss
Film Poster, 2005

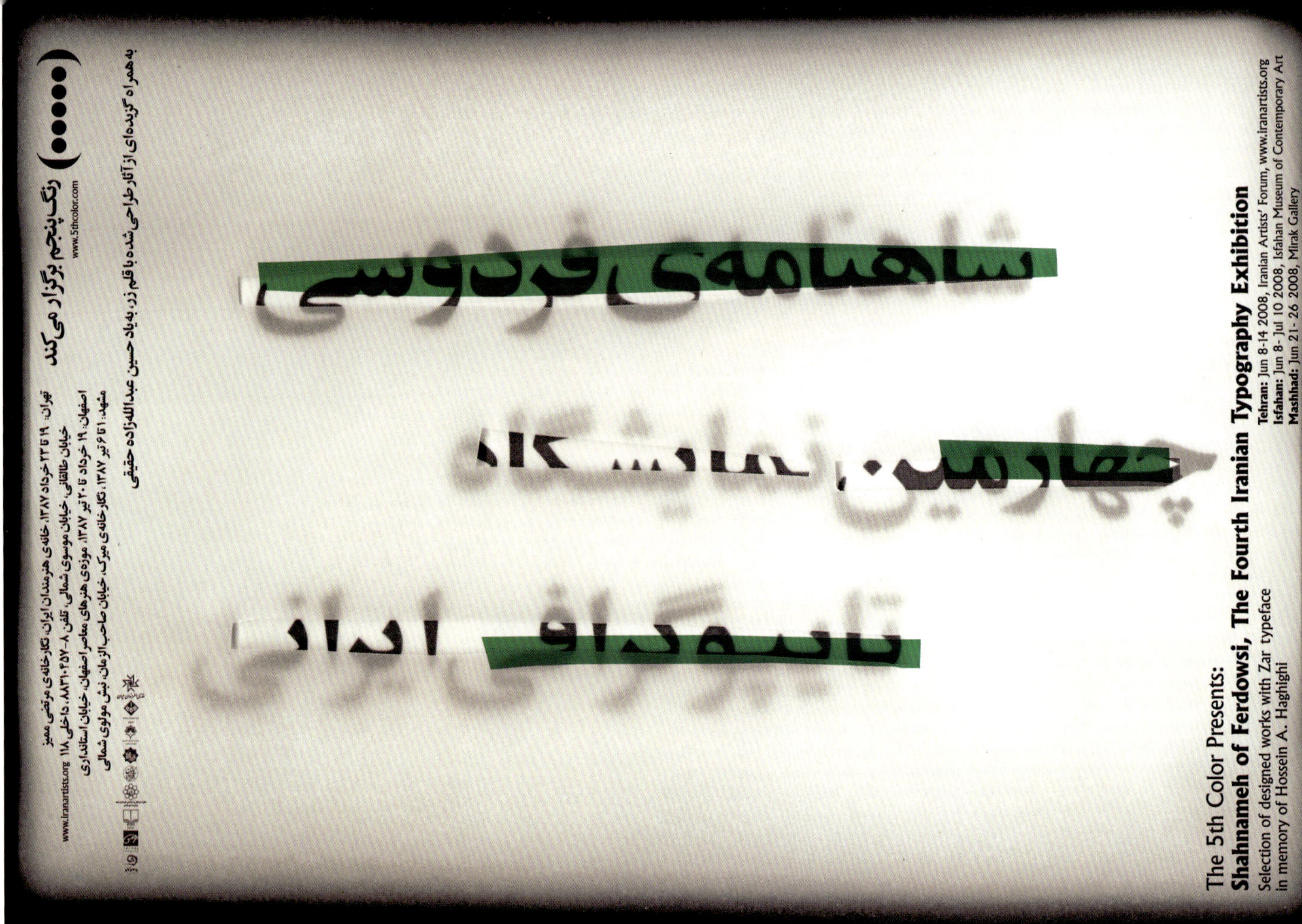

The Fourth Iranian Typography Exhibition
Poster, 2008

Cinema Verite,
The First Iran International Documentary Film Festival
Poster, 2007

Fifty-Fifty
The 5th Colour Exhibition in Italy
Poster, 2005

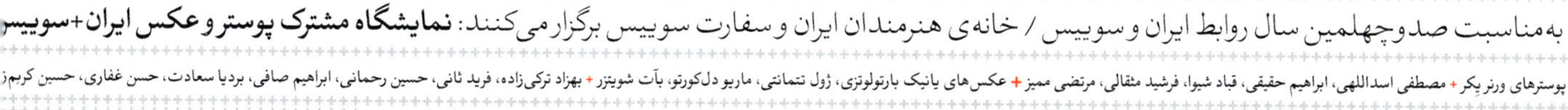

به‌مناسبت صدوچهلمین سال روابط ایران و سوییس / خانه‌ی هنرمندان ایران و سفارت سوییس برگزار می‌کنند: نمایشگاه مشترک پوستر و عکس ایران+سوییس
پوسترهای ورنر یکر + مصطفی اسداللهی، ابراهیم حقیقی، قباد شیوا، فرشید مثقالی، مرتضی ممیز + عکس‌های یانیک بارتولوتزی، ژول تتمانتی، ماریو دل‌کورتو، بآت شویتزر + بهزاد ترکی‌زاده، فرید ثانی، حسین رحمانی، ابراهیم صافی، بردیا سعادت، حسن غفاری، حسین کریم
جمعه ۱۴ تیرماه ۱۳۹۲ ساعت ۱۷ / تهران، خیابان طالقانی، خیابان شهید موسوی شمالی، باغ هنر، خانه‌ی هنرمندان ایران / تالار استاد شهناز

Switzerland.
To celebrate 140 years of friendship between Switzerland and Iran, The Embassy of Switzerland & The Iranian Artists Forum Present:
A Visual Dialogue between Switzerland + Iran
Friday, 5 July 2013 at 17:00 / Iranian Artists Forum, Auditorium Master Jalil Shahnaz (North Mousavi Str., Taleghani Ave, Tehran)

A Visual Dialogue Between Iran and Switzerland
Poster, 2013

GREG MORE

— Australia —

GREG MORE

Founder of the Melbourne-based studio OOM Creative, Greg More is an expert in data visualisations that connect art, design and technology.

A designer who was trained in architecture, Greg works with data, aesthetics and code to generate new ways of understanding information and provide clarity to complex situations.

Projects include visualisations for HSBC that allow currency data and exchange rates to be viewed on laptops, iPads and mobile phones. In conjunction with Melbourne Water, the studio has designed a series of data visualisations to illustrate water as an urban resource.

For the City of Melbourne, one project visualises pedestrian movements tracked on sensors located around the city so they can be monitored online.

Another visualises the database of trees in Melbourne's inner-city precincts as an interactive public map.

Greg is also working with the Melbourne Symphony Orchestra to visualise audience, ticketing and repertoire data.

His design work has been exhibited at the Museum of Modern Art New York, selected for OneDotZero and Resfest International Film Festivals, and featured in a range of international biennales, exhibitions and publications.

Greg is also a senior lecturer at the Spatial Information Architecture Laboratory within the School of Architecture & Design at RMIT University, Melbourne.

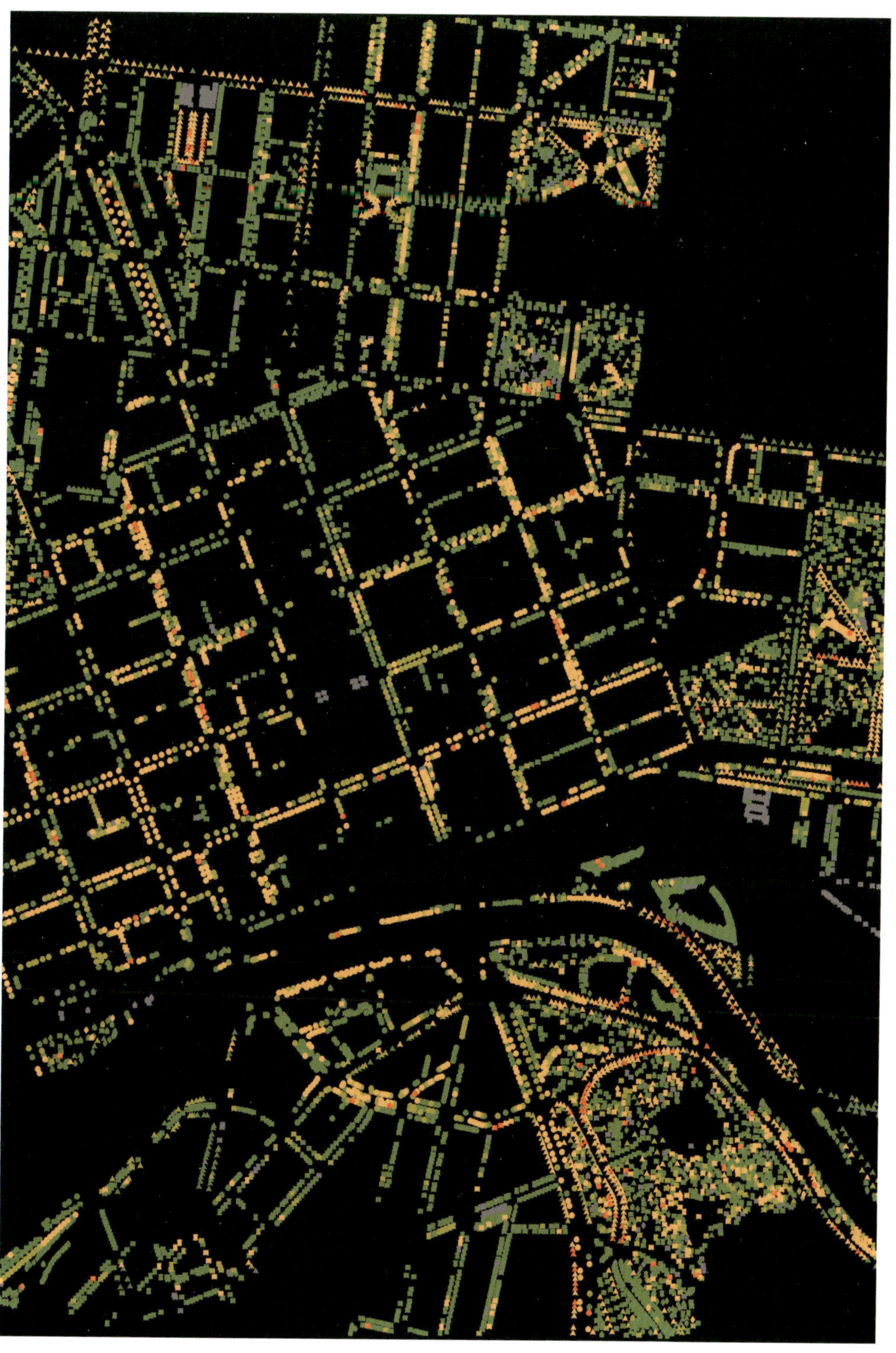

Visualising Melbourne's Urban Forest
2013

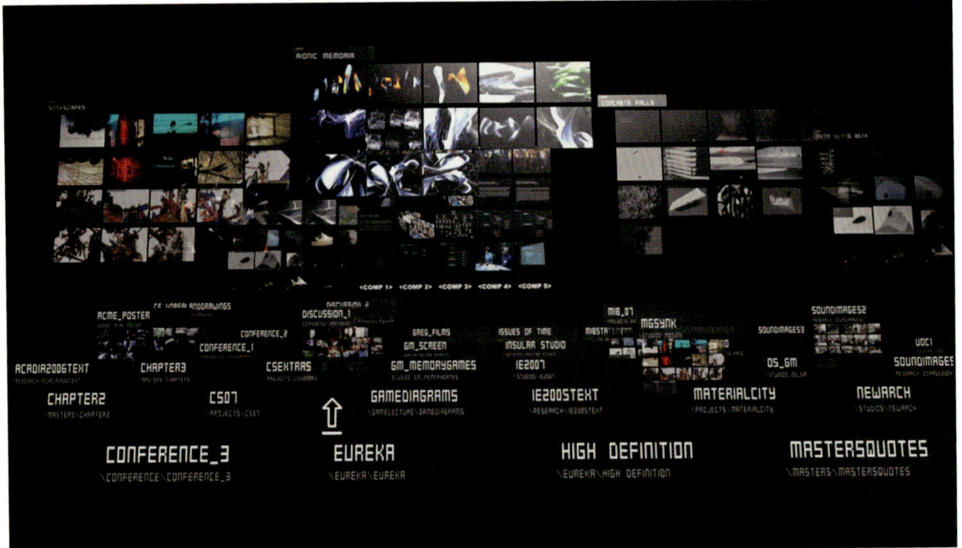

Eureka
Interactive presentation software
2002–2008

Thumpa

Digital film, 2003

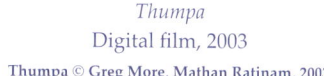

Thumpa © Greg More, Mathan Ratinam, 2003

Synthetic Environments
2008

Make Change
Data visualisation installation, 2010

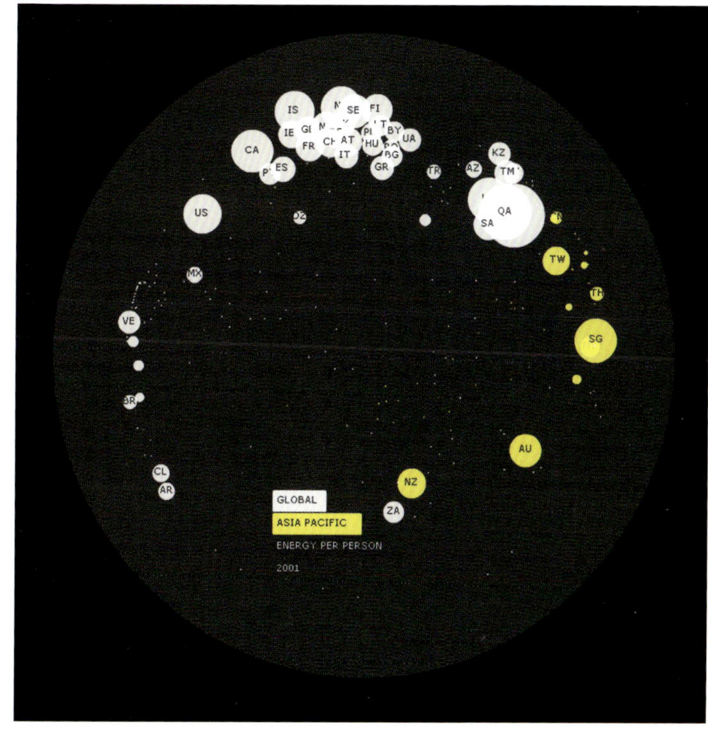

ALISON PAGE

— Australia —

ALISON PAGE

A descendant of the Walbanga and Wadi Wadi people of the Yuin nation, Alison Page is an award-winning designer and executive officer of the Saltwater Freshwater Arts Alliance.

Exploring links between cultural identity, art and design, her work spans architecture, interiors, jewellery and public art.

Since 1997, in association with Merrima Design, Alison has worked with various urban and rural Aboriginal communities in the delivery of culturally appropriate architectural and design services.

The Arts Alliance, based on the mid north coast of New South Wales, is governed by ten local Aboriginal land councils and hosts a range of cultural programs including the annual Saltwater Freshwater Festival and the National Aboriginal Design Agency.

Alison is also a board member of the Indigenous Land Corporation and Ninti One Ltd and for eight years was a regular panellist on the ABC TV program 'The New Inventors'.

In 2011, she was appointed by the Prime Minister to the Expert Panel for the Constitutional Recognition of Indigenous People.

Alison was named the Female Regional/ Rural Entrepreneur Manager of the Year in the NAB Women's Agenda Leadership Awards 2013 and was listed by respected online magazine Crikey as one of the 'top ten women to watch'.

The Sit Place
Australian Design Centre Interior, 2013

String Theory Pop Up Shop
Museum Contemporary Art Interior
Sydney, 2013
© NADA, 2013

The Sit Place
Australian Design Centre Interior, 2013
© NADA, 2013

NADA Bag
Product Design, 2013

Diamond Dreaming Range
Jewellery, 2007

SØREN INGOMAR PETERSEN

— USA —

SØREN INGOMAR PETERSEN

As an engineer, automotive designer and design researcher, Søren Petersen assists top-tier international organisations to translate business ideas into actionable design concepts for sustainable progress.

Since founding his consulting firm ingomar&ingomar in California in 1993, Søren has worked with BMW Group, DesignworksUSA, Ramboll Group, the Institute of Chartered Accountants in England and Wales, Stanford University, Copenhagen Business School, Fraunhofer Institute, Delft University, Hong Kong Polytechnic University, Kookmin University and Hanyang University.

Søren has a PhD in Design Research from Stanford University, a Masters in Mechanical Engineering from The Technical University of Denmark and a Bachelor of Science in Transportation Design from the Art Centre College of Design.

His research areas are design strategy, methods and tools for bridging business and design using design quantification. This includes design & business model experimentation, design balanced scorecards, design driven portfolio management, inspirational design briefing, managing designers' risk attitude and crowdsourcing design research.

Over recent years, Søren has published dozens of scientific papers and more than one hundred articles on The Creative Economy, as well as authoring 'Profit from Design: Leveraging design in business', an inspiring new way of looking at design metrics. He publishes weekly in The Huffington Post on The Creative Economy.

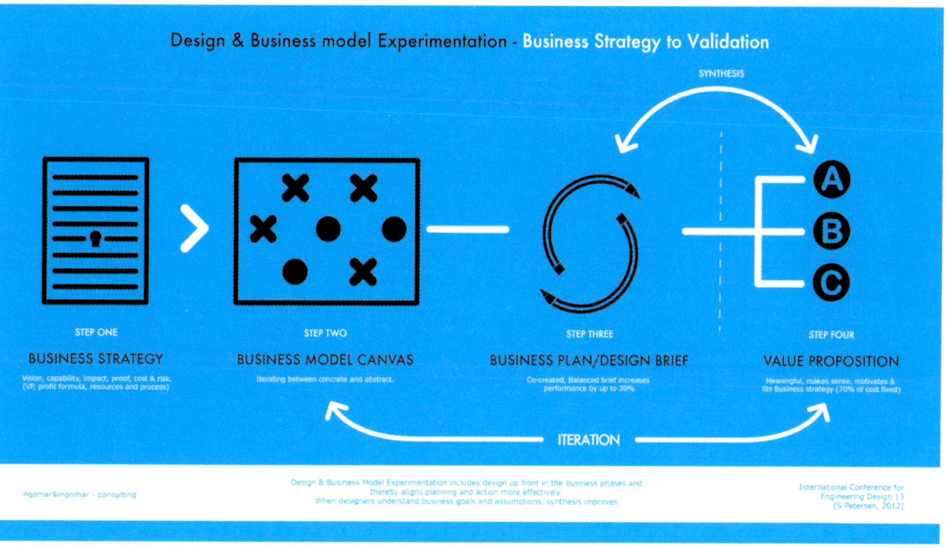

Design and Business model Experimentation
International Conference for
Engineering and Design, 13

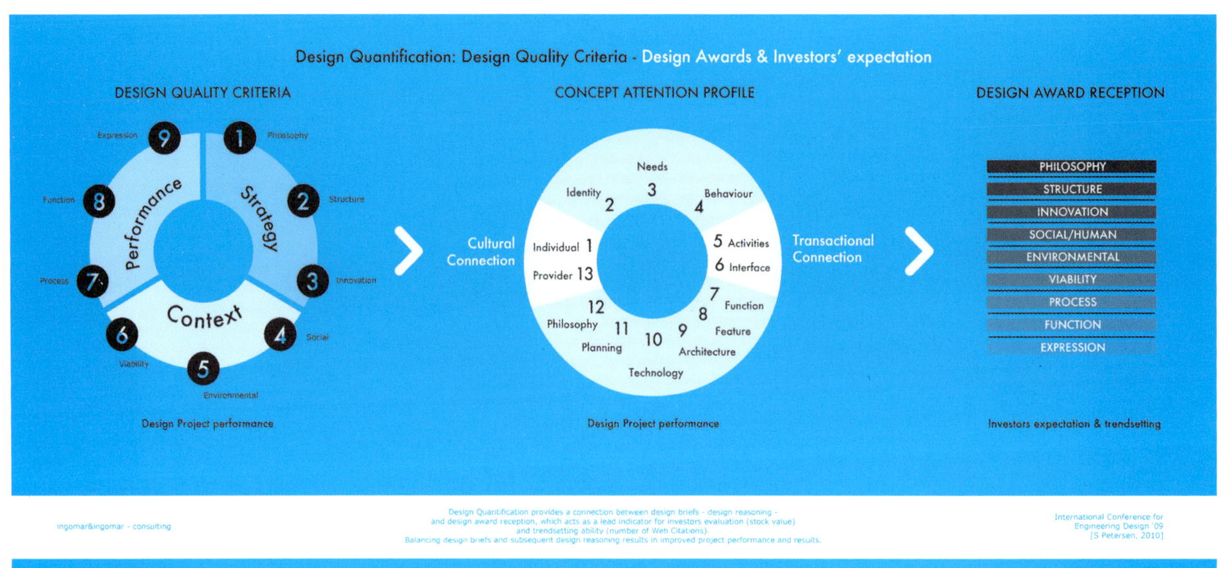

Design Quantification: Design Quality Criteria
International Conference for Engineering Design '09
© S Petersen, 2010

Insirational Design Briefing

Stanford and Industry study

© S Petersen, 2010

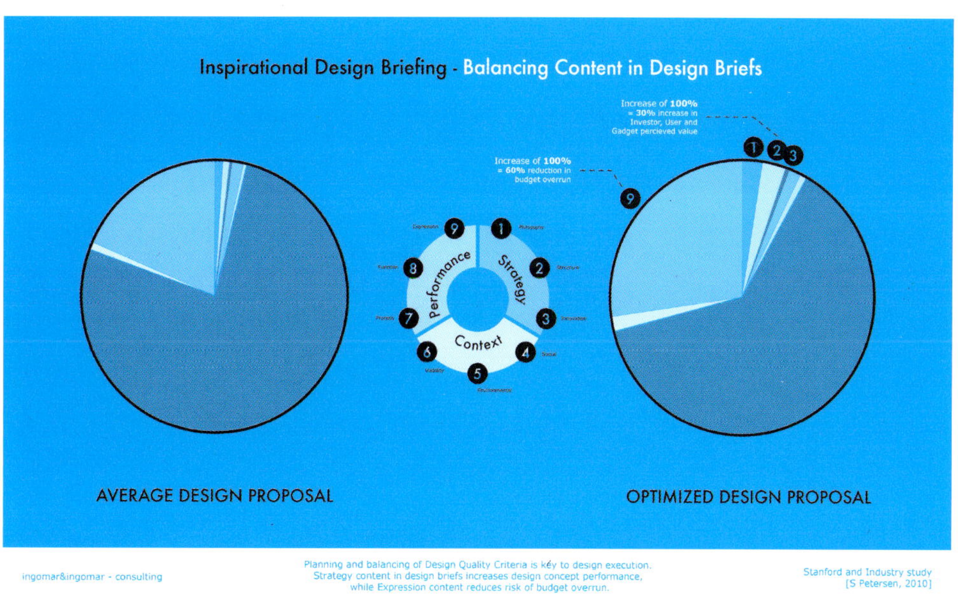

Design Quantification: Concept Attention Profile
International Conference for Engineering
Design '05

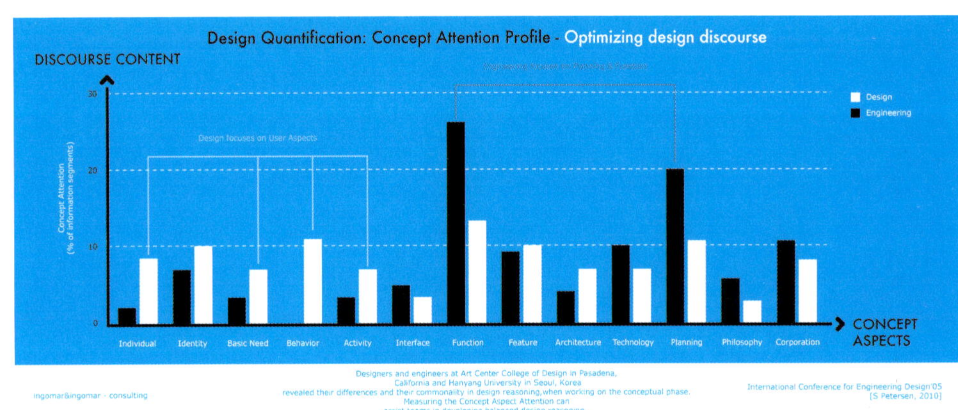

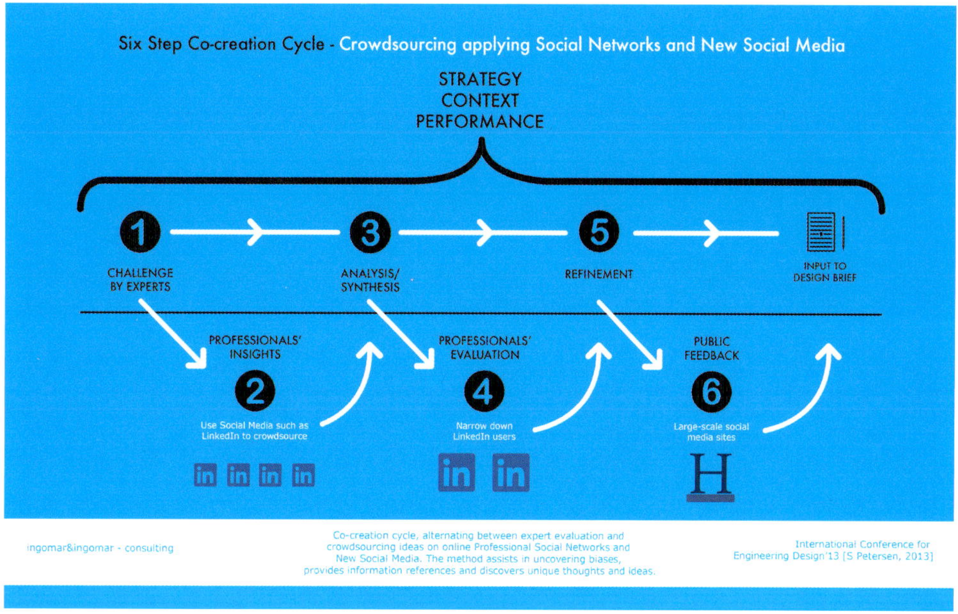

Six Step Co-creation Cycle
International Conference for Engineering Design '13
© S Petersen, 2013

DAVID RETALLACK

— Australia —

DAVID RETALLACK

David Retallack's designs have thrilled billions of people worldwide. The general manager of FCT Flames in Adelaide, he designs and builds Olympic flames.

David's job is to craft an invisible gas into an exciting, spellbinding experience that bursts into life at one exact moment, without fail. With the whole world watching, there are no second chances. Fire is one of the most basic of elements and taming it is the key.

Trained as a mechanical engineer with experience in combustion and high temperature processes, David entered this highly specialised realm in the lead-up to the Sydney 2000 Olympics. He and his team of designers and engineers are now world leaders in their field.

David takes creating spectacular flame effects, such as flames burning on water, in his stride. Working with the world's leading designers of opening ceremonies, including Australians Rick Birch and David Atkins, he interprets their intent for the look, feel and emotional impact of the flame and then designs and builds the burners and cauldrons.

David is now leading FCT Flames into the production of spectacular flame features for temporary and permanent installations, as well as continuing to be involved in the Olympics and other major sporting event ceremonies.

Games Cauldron
Rio de Janeiro, 2007
FCT Flames, © Brad Wilson, 2007

Athens 2004 Olympic Games
Opening Ceremony
Special flame effect on water, 2004
Getty Images, ©Donald Miralle, 2004

Athens 2004 Olympic Games,
Torch Relay
Olympic Games Torch, 2004
FCT Flames, ©Brad Wilson, 2004

Beijing 2008 Olympic Games
Equestrian Competition
Olympic Cauldron, 2008
FCT Flames, ©Nader Qamar, 2008

London 2012 Olympic Games
Opening Ceremony
Olympic Cauldron, 2012
Getty Images, ©AFP, 2012

HANNAH ROSE ROBINSON

— Australia —

HANNAH ROSE ROBINSON

Hannah Rose Robinson is a freelance photographer from Newcastle who's been attracting accolades for her commercial and documentary work.

While her commercial photography is a marriage of fashion, lifestyle and quirky portraiture, Hannah's documentary work explores stories of everyday life in Australia and abroad, with a particular interest in nomadic cultures.

Hannah was a finalist in the Olive Cotton Portrait Prize 2009 and The National Portrait Prize 2010, a runner up in the Moran Contemporary Photographic Prize 2010 and was named Emerging Editorial Photographer of the Year by ACMP Trampoline in 2010.

That year Hannah shot 'The Empire', an intimate exploration of the bond shared by a group of homeless men in her home town, presented at the Australian Centre for Photography and Reportage Projections.

In 2012, she journeyed across the wild east of Mongolia on horseback, documenting the local culture for her film 'The Last Nomad', which subsequently featured at the 2013 Reportage Festival Projections and the 2013 HeadON Photography Festival.

After completing the film Hannah attended a Reflexions world masterclass in Europe and has recently returned from four months shooting stories in the USA, Mexico, Central America and Cuba. Her upcoming work is focused on rural Australia.

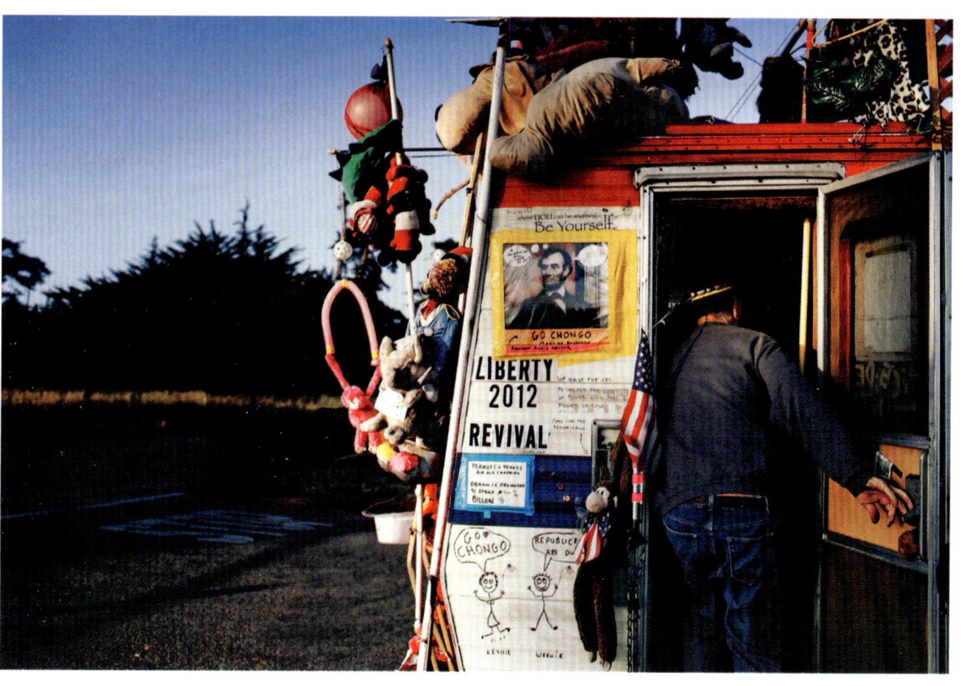

From 'Little America'
Photograph, 2012

From 'The Last Nomad'
Photographic Essay, 2011

From 'The Empire'
Photographic Essay, 2009

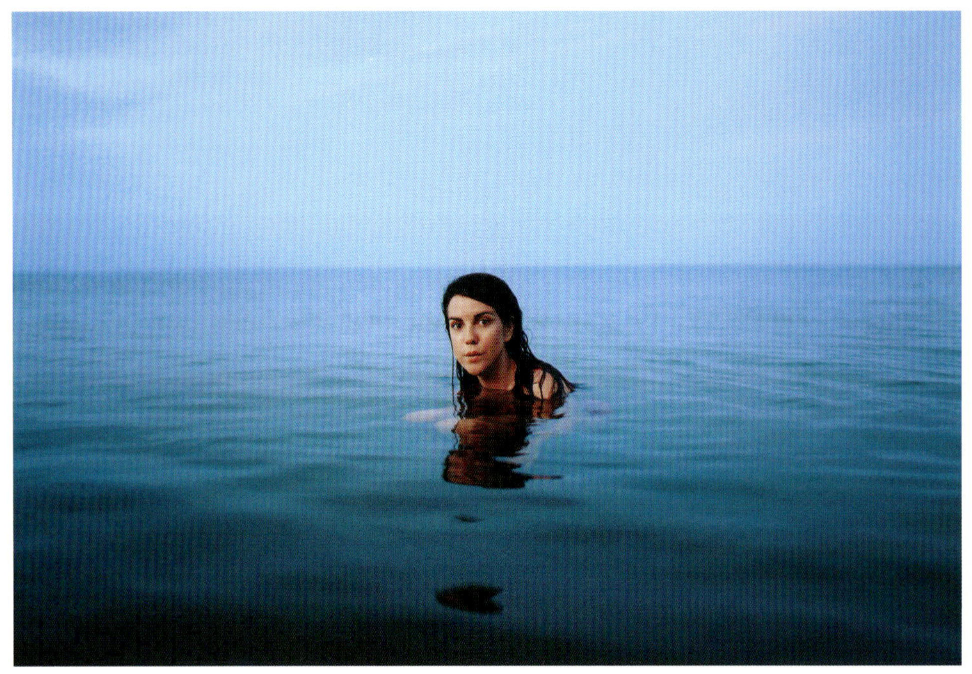

From 'The Island of Youth'
Photograph, 2012

House of Elsmore Editorial
Photograph, 2013

STUDIO ROOSEGAARDE

— Netherlands —

STUDIO ROOSEGAARDE

The social design lab Studio Roosegaarde, named after founder Daan Roosegaarde delivers unimaginable technology to the world – in the most literal way. With studio's in Rotterdam and Shanghai, we develop innovative, interactive landscapes that are accomplished through the objective of pulling technology 'out of the screen' and integrating it into the real world.

Studio Roosegaarde believes the key to accomplishing this, is our Dutch attitude of artist-entrepreneur, which considers equal parts "priest and entrepreneur" in order to perfectly merge technology and creativity. Through the creation of social designs that instinctively respond to sound and movement, Studio Roosegaarde is able to pursue the widest possibilities of technological innovation.

Our professional mission is to create the missing links between bullshit and beauty, between fantasy and budget. We believes that The Netherlands must lose its "yes, but..." attitude and "look for the missing links". This link between between ideology and technology, is what Daan Roosegaarde calls "techno-poetry".

Marbles
Molded shapes, waterproof casing, including LEDs, sensor technology and sound speakers
Almere, Netherlands, 2012

Smart Highway
Smart paints, energy harvesting, sensors 2012–2015
© Studio Roosegaarde and Heijmans

Dune
Fibers, LEDs, sensors, speakers, interactive
software and electronics
2006–2001

Intimacy 2.0
Smart foils, wireless technologies,
electronics, LEDs and copper, 2010–2011
© Studio Roosegaarde

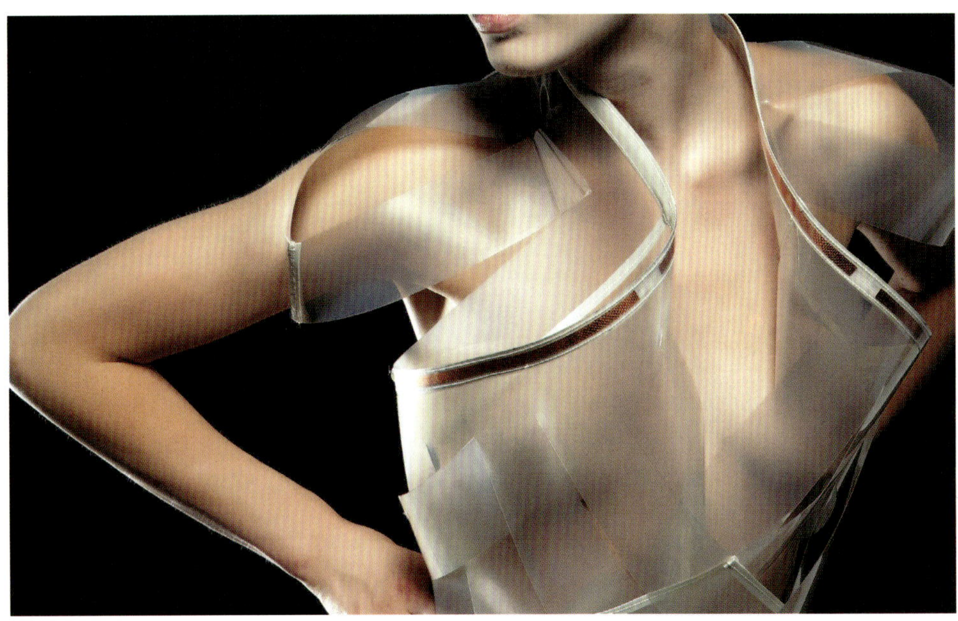

Lotus Dome
Smart foils, lamps, sensors, software
Commissioned by City of Lille for Lille3000
Fantastic exhibition, 2010–2011

KENT SNEDDON

— New Zealand —

KENT SNEDDON

As design director of the global bathroom products group Methven, Kent Sneddon plays a key role in driving the product concepts and brand-building initiatives of this progressive design-led company.

Since joining Methven in 2006, Kent has built the design team that has developed many innovative technologies, shower products and tapware collections, along with future concepts yet to enter the market.

After graduating from Wellington School of Design in 1994, Kent worked with noted designer Peter Haythornthwaite on various projects ranging from packaging and signage to electronic products and tools.

He then moved to Fisher & Paykel and went on to lead the development of a global strategy for a new generation of appliances and concepts for the company.

During his time at Methven, the design team has won many prestigious awards including Red Dot Design Awards (Germany), German Design Council Awards, Good Design Awards (USA), a Good Design Green Award (USA), UK Designer Awards, Australian International Design Awards and NZ Best Design Awards.

A member of the Designers Institute of New Zealand, Kent has been a member of the advisory board of Unitec Institute of Technology and the AUT School of Art and Design and has judged numerous design competitions.

Satinjet Kiri Shower System and Tapware
Product Design, 2010

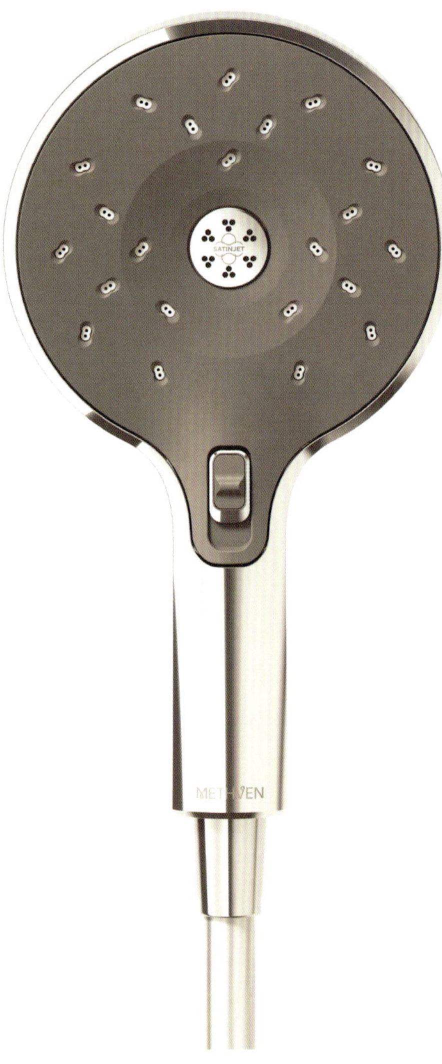

Satinjet Kaha Shower
Product Design, 2013

Satinjet Tahi Shower System
Product Design, 2010

Satinjet Kiri Shower Spray
Product Design, 2010

Aroha Tapware
Product Design, 2012

SUPER CRITICAL MASS

— Australia —

SUPER CRITICAL MASS

Reconnecting yourself to your sonic body, to the acoustic and lived environment, and to a relational community. Such is the practice of Super Critical Mass (SCM) and its three directors Julian Day, Luke Jaaniste and Janet McKay.

Since 2008 they've been creating sound 'masses' in cities across Australia and around the world, with each mass using one type of sound source to generate an evolving ambient field in a participatory creative process.

SCM has enlivened parklands, laneways, cathedrals, industrial buildings and galleries, using such sound sources as woodwind, brass, percussion, found objects and ready-mades.

Highlights include 'Swelter' for brass players surrounding the lake in New York's Central Park, the 'Soundland' project, which activated the steel skeleton of the old Cockatoo Island industrial zone, and 'Voices' for communal singers within the stone chasm of Manchester Cathedral.

They've also been in residence at Arts House and Federation Square in Melbourne, and with CUSP, the Australian Design Centre's touring exhibition of design into the next decade.

Beyond SCM, the directors pursue their own practice. Julian is a composer, visual artist and radio broadcaster, Luke a sonic and visual artist and philosophical writer, and Janet a flautist, music educator and new music event producer.

Luke Jaaniste, Julian Day and Janet McKay
Photo by Dan Cole

Aura
Sound and visual exhibition
Aurora Festival, Blacktown Arts Centre, 2012
Wall images shot by Alex Wisser, Photo by Luke Jaaniste

Critical Mass
Flute mass, CarraigeWorks Sydney, 2008
Photo by Dominik Krupinski

Slope
Bell mass, Audio Architecture
Melbourne Arts Centre, 2012
Photo by Ava Rose

Soundland
Mass for wood and steel
Underbelly Lab and Festival
Cockatoo Island, 2013
Photo by Hospital Hill

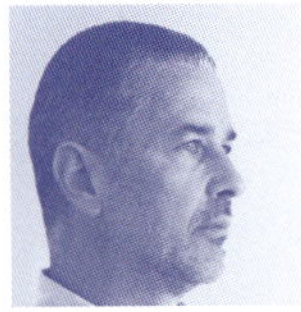

PAOLO TASSINARI

— Italy —

PAOLO TASSINARI

Paolo Tassinari is a partner in the Tassinari/Vetti design studio in Trieste, long known for its outstanding work in the fields of editorial design, visual identity, communication and exhibition design.

Co-founded by Paolo in 1985, the studio works mainly for public institutions, museums, major exhibitions and cultural events.

Identity and communication projects have recently been developed for the National Museum of the Palace of Versailles, Palacongressi of Rimini, Palazzo Grassi and Punta della Dogana at Venice, Rome Archeological Heritage Service, the Naples Theatre Festival, the New Archeological Museum of Reggio Calabria, the Modern and Contemporary Art Museum of Palazzo Belmonte Riso in Palermo, Friuli Venezia Giulia Region, Rome Modern Art National Gallery, the Venice Biennale and Milan Triennale.

Paolo was awarded the prestigious Compasso d'Oro/Assocation of Industrial Design prize in 2011 for the visual identity of the Naples Theatre Festival.

He is also art director of the international architecture magazine Casabella and art director of the art and architectural branch of the publishing house Electa.

A member of Alliance Graphique Internationale since 2006, Paolo has been visiting professor at Trieste University, is currently teaching at the Polytechnic School of Design in Milan, and is co-author of 'Sussidario', published in 2011.

Foto/Industria Photography Biennale
Poster Design, 2013

Banca Patrimoni Sella & C
Environmental graphics, 2013
Photo © ORCH Alessandra Chemollo

Casabella
Magazine cover, 2013

Foto/Industria Photography Biennale
Catalogues design, 2013

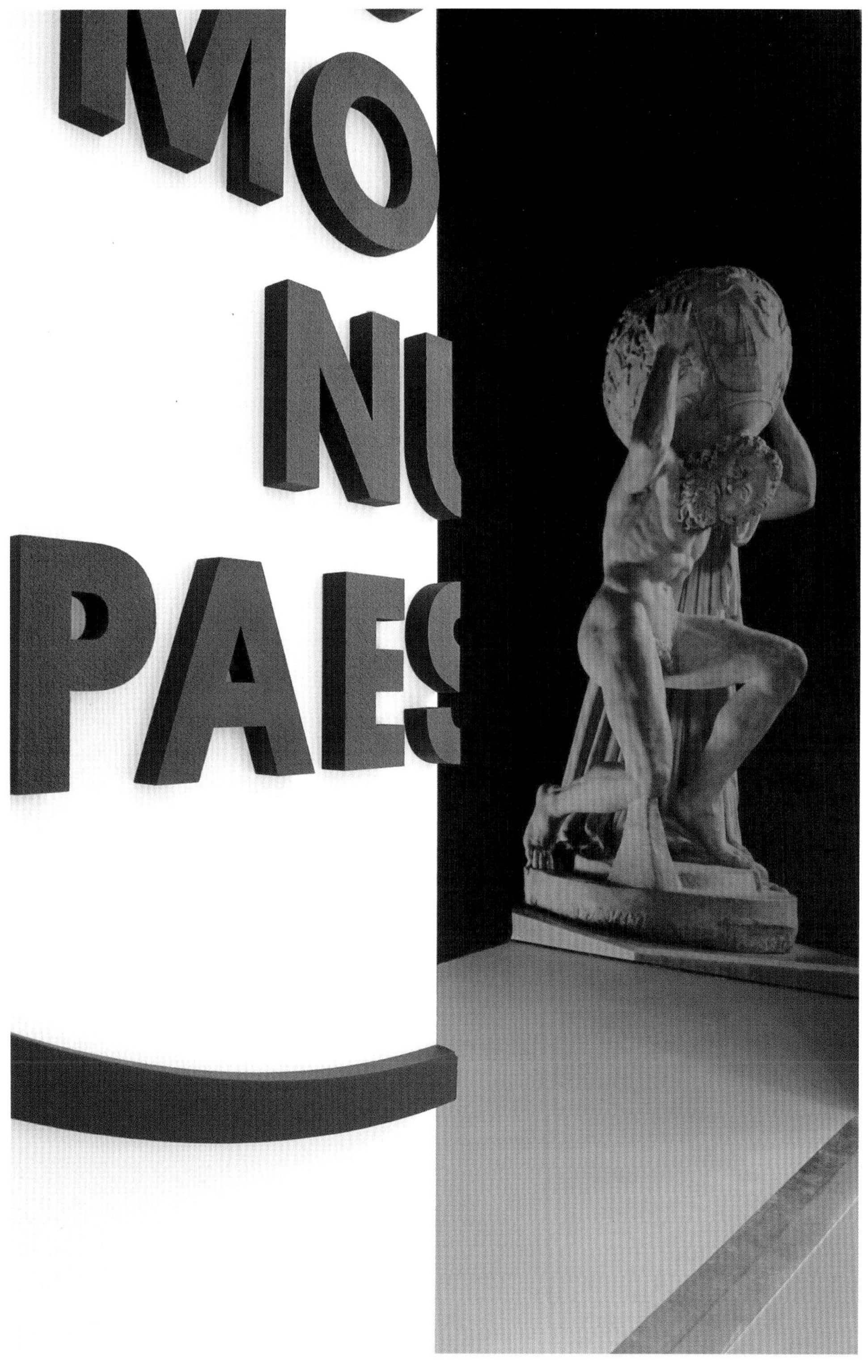

L'architettura del Mondo
Exhibition identity and graphics, 2012

MARI VELONAKI

— Greece —

MARI VELONAKI

Mari Velonaki is an artist and researcher in the field of interactive installation art, creating works that incorporate movement, speech, touch, breath, electrostatic charge, artificial vision and robotics.

She commenced practice in 1997 and is currently associate professor and director of the Creative Robotics Lab at the National Institute of Experimental Arts at the College of Fine Arts, The University of New South Wales.

In 2003 Mari initiated and led a major art/science project 'Fish–Bird: Autonomous Interactions in a Contemporary Arts Setting 2004–2007' for the Australian Research Council in collaboration with roboticists at the Australian Centre for Field Robotics.

In 2006 she co-founded the Centre for Social Robotics, dedicated to inter-disciplinary research into human-robot interaction in spaces that incorporate the general public.

Mari was awarded an Australia Council Visual Arts Fellowship in 2007 and, in 2009, a four-year Australia Research Council Queen Elizabeth II Fellowship to develop a project aimed at understanding the physicality that is possible and acceptable between a human and a robot.

Mari's artworks have been exhibited at major museums and festivals throughout Australia and in New Zealand, the UK, China, Korea, Denmark, the USA, Spain, Austria and Germany.

Current State of Affairs (detail)
Responsive Installation
(Electricity, water, sound generation)

Diamandini
Robotic Inteactive Installation
Image courtesy of the Victoria & Albert museum

Fish-Bird
Robotic Interactive Installation
© Mari Velonaki

Circle D: Fragile Balances (detail)
Interactive objects

Circle E: Fragile Balances
Interactive object

ROBBIE WELLS

— New Zealand —

ROBBIE WELLS

Robbie Wells is a director of 4DESIGN in Sydney, an industrial design and product development firm recognised internationally for its creativity and market-driven approach to design.

An industrial designer for more than 20 years, Robbie co-founded the consultancy in 2003, specialising in the design, engineering and manufacture of consumer and commercial products.

The firm has specific expertise in developing technically demanding products for the medical, consumer, mining, defence, commercial, transportation and infrastructure industries.

Their clients include Qantas, Dell, Transport for NSW, Hewlett-Packard, Westinghouse, GE, IBM, Microsoft, AtCor Medical, BT Imaging Systems, Sony, XBox, Insight Sport Technology and Sunbeam.

Robbie and his team believe in a hands-on approach to product development and have extensive in-house prototype facilities, including 3D printing.

While maintaining a traditional approach to concept development by means of sketch, CAD and physical modelling, they have also embraced industry-leading surfacing software to facilitate complex product solutions.

Since being established, 4DESIGN has developed more than 200 products, been extensively awarded by the world's leading design authorities, and set up a second office, in Queenstown, New Zealand.

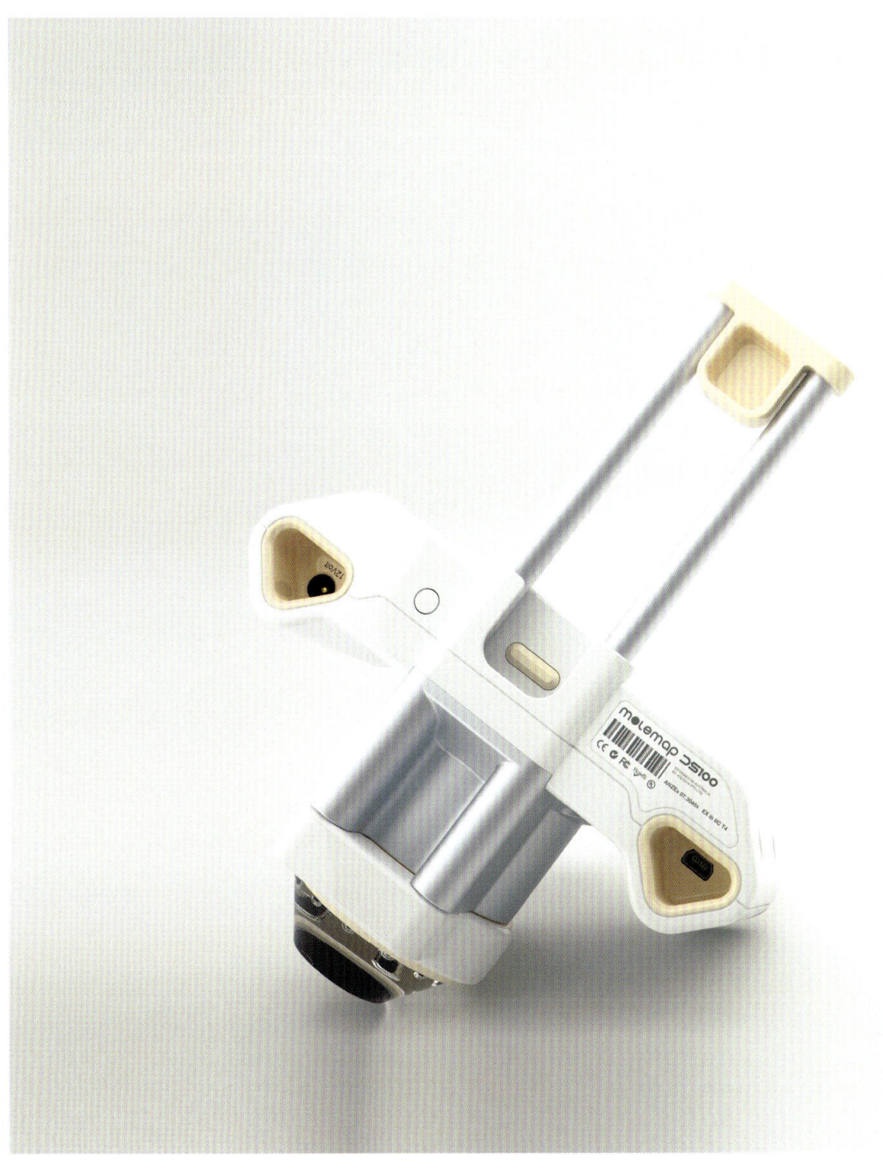

MoleMap
Medical Digital Camera, 2010
© **4design**

HUB MFP
Multi-function street Pole system, 2005
© **4design**

L5
Digital Lighting Controller, 2011
© 4design

MLP 6A
Power distribution system, 2009

Emotiv Insight
Wireless Headset for
brainwave reading, 2013
© **4design**

CHARLES WILSON

— Australia —

CHARLES WILSON

One of Australia's most celebrated industrial designers, Charles Wilson co-founded the Sydney-based Argo collective to develop experimental furniture and decorative objects.

Set up in 1991, it was with Argo that Charles designed the CW1 Swivel Chair for Woodmark, the first of many successful production designs.

He has gone on to win a number of design awards, including The Australian Design Award for his Candelabra by Menu, The Bombay Sapphire Award for his 'Spool' seating, and Launchpad Design of the Year.

His Swivel Chair and Candelabra by Menu are in the permanent design collection of Sydney's Powerhouse Museum.

Public commissions include a furniture suite and side tables for the State Drawing Room of Government House, Sydney, and concepts for multifunction streetlight poles for Sydney City Council.

Recent projects include a blackwood tallboy for Broached Commissions and a swivel chair for Herman Miller. Exhibited at Design Days, Dubai, in 2012, the Broached tallboy was cited by Wallpaper magazine as 'one of the most sophisticated pieces in the fair'.

In 2013, Charles's Serif stools were exhibited in the Salon de Mobile at the Temporary Museum of New Design, Milan, and were shown at 100% Design, London, the UK's largest contemporary design event for industry professionals.

George
Lounge chair and ottoman for
King Furniture, 2013

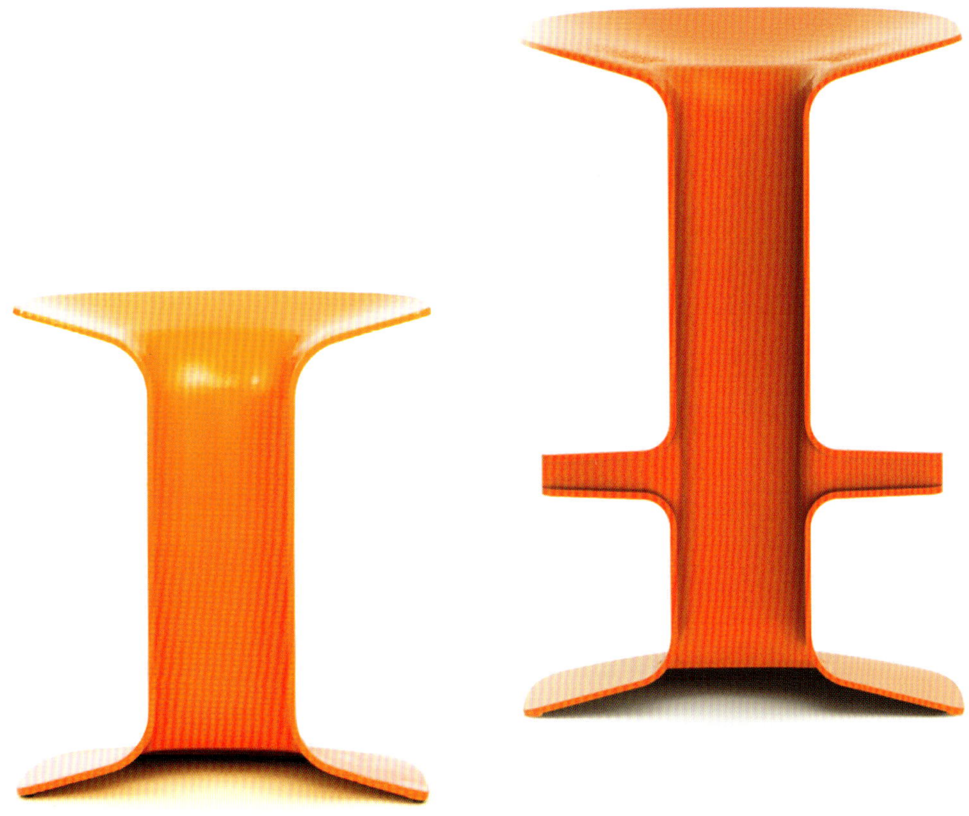

SERIF STOOLS
Aluminium stools, 2012

CP1 SOFA
Sofa range for
Woodmark, 2001

TALLBOY
Blackwood Tallboy for
The Broached Commission
© **Felix Forest**

MENU KANDELABER
Nickel candelabra designed for
Danish brand Menu, 2005

ALLA WOLF-TASKER AM

— Australia —

ALLA WOLF-TASKER AM

Alla Wolf-Tasker is the proprietor and culinary director of Lake House, the famed boutique hotel and restaurant in the 'spa' town of Daylesford, Victoria.

An icon in Australian regional dining, Alla opened Lake House more than 30 years ago with husband Allan and it has attracted acclamation and awards ever since.

Recent accolades include listings in Tatler's Top 100 Hotels in the world and Australia's Hottest 50 Restaurants, Australia's Best Country Winelist, and the Best of Excellence Award from NY Wine Spectator.

Widely acknowledged for her pioneering work in establishing regional destination dining in Australia, Alla was championing local seasonal cuisine long before it became a marketing mantra.

Her tenacity and belief in what was possible and her work with small-scale producers, often providing a voice for the unsung suppliers of the culinary world, is legendary.

As well as running Lake House, Alla is an author; ambassador for good food, sustainability and best practise; public speaker; educator; mentor to a generation of young industry professionals; and hero to a long list of self-confessed food lovers.

Alla has been recognised with two Living Legend Awards and was honoured in 2007 with an Order of Australia for her services to tourism and the hospitality industry.

Daylesford Winter, Carrot, chestnut, pumpkin, kale, currants, grain, seed
Food Design

Apple, buttermilk, honey, walnut, oatmeal
Food design
© Alla Wolf-Tasker and Lake House

Peanut butter, black sesame, caramel, banana
Food Design
© Alla Wolf-Tasker and Lake House

The Lake House

© Alla Wolf-Tasker and Lake House

Free range chicken, poached and in ravioli, morels, nettle, truffle, champagne sabayon
Food Design

KONGJIAN YU

— *China* —

KONGJIAN YU

Renowned as the pre-eminent contemporary landscape designer in China, Kongjian Yu is founder and president of the architecture, landscape architecture and urban design firm Turenscape.

Defining landscape and urban design as the 'art of survival', he is well known for elegant solutions with a strong environmental stance that sensitively integrate with their surroundings.

Kongjian's ecological approach to urbanism has been implemented in more than 200 cities in China and abroad, being recognised with many national honors.

He also has won numerous industry awards, including the Urban Land Institute Global Award for Excellence, multiple American Society of Landscape Architects Awards of Excellence and Honour Awards, and three Landscape of the Year awards from the World Architecture Festival.

The founder and dean of the College of Architecture and Landscape at Peking University, Kongjian received his doctorate in design from the Harvard Graduate School of Design and is a fellow of American Society of Landscape Architects.

He lectures worldwide and has recently served on the juries for the Aga Kahn Architecture Award and the World Architecture Festival.

Kongjian has produced several books and his life and work is documented in the monograph 'Designed Ecologies: The Landscape Architecture of Kongjian Yu', published in 2012.

Halleluja Concert Hall
Architecture as landscape harmonizing
man and nature, 2010
©Kongjian Yu & Turenscape

Tianjin Bridged Gardens
Gathering space created in a former brownfield landscape architecture, 2009
©Kongjian Yu & Turenscape

Qunli stormwater park
Landscape as green sponge for water resilient city, landscape architecture, 2012
©Kongjian Yu & Turenscape

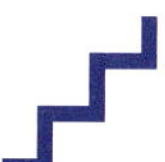

Tianjin Qiaoyuan wetland park
Low maintenance park,
landscape architecture,2009
©Kongjian Yu & Turenscape

Qian'an Sanlihe Greenway
A mother recovered by integrating
ecology and art, landscape architecture, 2011

JONATHAN ZAWADA

— Australia / USA —

ZAWADA JONATHAN

Born in Perth and currently living and working in Los Angeles, Jonathan Zawada is a multifaceted designer and artist whose approach has been described as 'corporate dada'.

He has become best known for his varied approach to the discipline of design, working across many different mediums and visual styles including music, fashion and publishing.

Jonathan has worked with companies such as Bloomberg, Nike, BMW, Herman Miller, Asos and Warp Records, and exhibited in Los Angeles, Sydney, Barcelona and Paris.

His art practice is informed by his early roots in web design, coding and animation and by his further evolution into commercial graphic design, illustration and art direction. He now also works in object design, sculpture, video, installation and painting.

Jonathan's art and design has been recognised with an Aria, a Bronze D&AD award and a Museums Australia Multimedia and Publication Design Award.

Flight 77
Oil on canvas, 2011

Herman Miller, Then X Ten

Poster, 2012

Chester French, MUSIC 4 TNGRS
Album Cover, 2012

The Presets, Pacifica
Album Cover, 2012

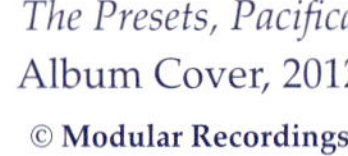

TRU$T FUN!
Promotional image, Art Direction, 2009

DESIGN DIRECTORY

DESIGN DIRECTORY

AUSTRALIAN TAPESTRY WORKSHOP

austapestry.com.au

Eye desire
Sally Smart, 2011
Woven by Sue Batten and Chris Cochius
Photo: Viki Petherbridge

Rome
Frent Harris, 2012
Photo: Jeremy Weihrauch

Studio floor at the ATW's heritage-listed building

The Australian Tapestry Workshop is an international leader in the art of contemporary tapestry. Established in 1976, it is the only workshop of its kind in Australia and one of a few in the world dedicated to the production of hand-woven tapestries. Artists worldwide are discovering how this traditional medium can be used in completely new ways, and the Workshop is in the vanguard of this revival.

The Workshop is one of Australia's leading producers of public art with tapestries at leading institutions such as the National Gallery of Australia, National Library, Sydney Opera House and Arts Centre Melbourne, as well as corporate and government locations and private residences. They also appear internationally including at eight Australian embassies.

C DESIGN STUDIO

cdesignstudio.com.au

Yacht Interior, Main Deck Saloon
Carly Thomas & Misha Merzliakov

Yacht Interior, Main Deck Lounge
Carly Thomas & Misha Merzliakov

C Design Studio is a multidisciplinary design studio offering professional, innovative and stylish design solutions.

C Design Studio offers a full design service from concept to production, using state of the art CAD programs.

Designer and proprietor Carly Thomas, graduated with an Advanced Diploma of Design for Industry from the Central Institute of Technology in Perth in 2003. In 2004 she was employed full time as a Designer/Stylist/Draftsperson by Austal, a world leader in aluminium vessel design and construction.

After almost eight years and many vessel designs completed, building on her experience in all fields of the design process, Carly decided it was time to establish her own design company, and C Design Studio was born.

CATO BRAND PARTNERS

catobrandpartners.com

Zhi Feng Tang, China
Identity, Packaging and Architectural Design

Since Cato Brand Partners was founded over forty years ago, the firm's design philosophy has remained the same, driving its expansion into a truly global design firm. Clients are now located in thirty-four countries and in every business sector. Approaching design projects on the basis of developing a 'Broader Visual Language™', the firm has greatly enhanced the ability of companies to build strong identities and brands that are visually distinctive, enduring and versatile. In this way, Cato Brand Partners helps companies create and apply visual communications that transcended cultural and language boundaries and stand out in the global marketplace. The potency of this all encompassing approach to design is enabling clients around the world to gain and maintain market leadership and maximize their business opportunities.

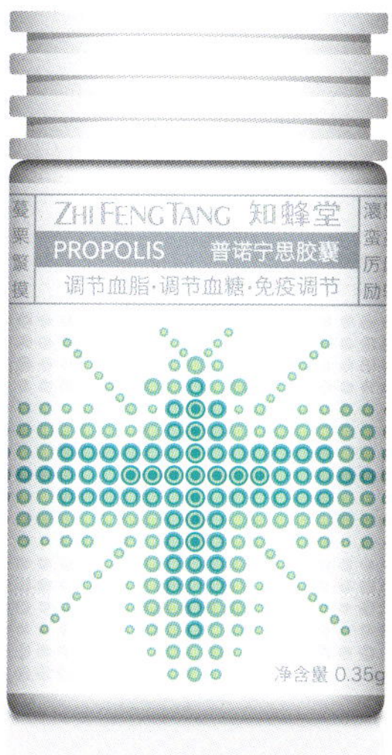
ZHI FENG TANG 知蜂堂
PROPOLIS 普诺宁思胶囊
调节血脂·调节血糖·免疫调节
净含量 0.35g

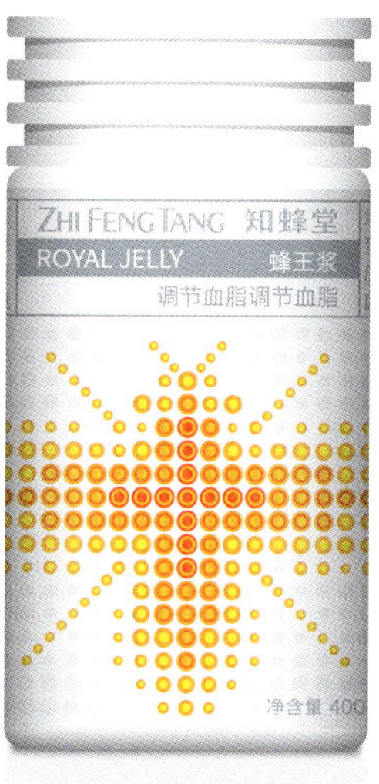
ZHI FENG TANG 知蜂堂
ROYAL JELLY 蜂王浆
调节血脂调节血脂

Henderson Global Investors, Spain
Identity

Group ADO, Mexico
Identity

Abu Dhabi Ship Building, United Arab Emirates
Brand Strategy and Identity

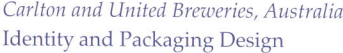

Carlton and United Breweries, Australia
Identity and Packaging Design

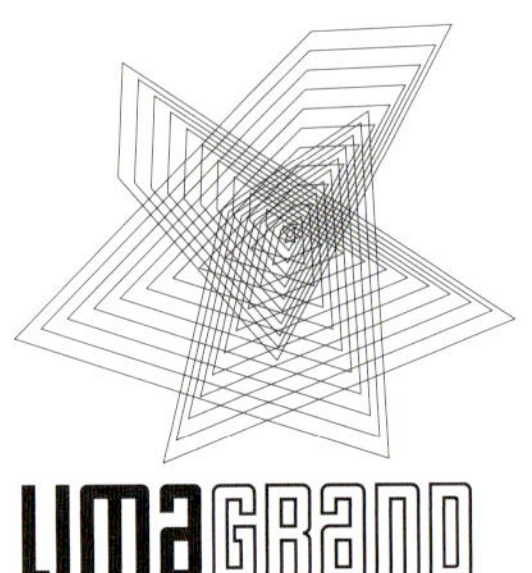

Group Interbank and URBI Properties, Peru
Brand Strategy and Identity

State Government of South Australia
Brand Strategy and Identity

WOMAD New Zealand
Identity

CMD
STRATEGY—DESIGN—INNOVATION

cmd.net.au

MAXTRAX MKII Recovery Boards
Industrial Design

Challenger Walk Behind mower
Rover Industrial Design

CMD is an acclaimed strategic design and innovation consultancy. We draw upon the pooled experience of a vibrant and creative team, that are some of the best industry talents in industrial, user experience, communication and strategic design.

We design great product and customer experiences.

With our clients, we use customer insight, collaboration and co-creation to create 'made magic' that makes a meaningful difference to the world.

Guest Lounge kiosk, Virgin Australia
Visualization renderings
Industrial Design

Guest Lounge kiosk, Virgin Australia
Industrial Design

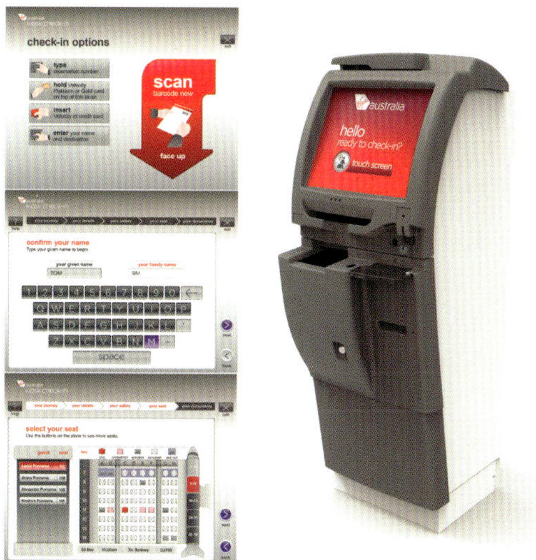

User Interface, Check In kiosk, Virgin Australia
UX and GUI

CORNWELL

cornwell.com.au

Ward Village, Hawaii
Place Making, Brand Strategy
Identity and Art Direction
Photo: Juli Balla

Cornwell has been establishing, building and communicating brands since our inception 20 years ago. Cornwell was founded in 1993 by Steve Cornwell and his wife Jane, and with their passion and skill for design they set about creating one of Australia's most recognised and awarded design studios. In 2004, Cornwell joined the STW Group, Australia's largest communications services group. With local, national and global recognition, Cornwell has developed a reputation for excellence.

Today, with over 30 design, creative, account service and digital professionals who bring an insightful and strategic focus to brand-oriented business issues, Cornwell has transitioned from a graphic design studio into a premium brand and communications agency.

SEE/CHANGE, South Street Seaport New York
Place Making, Brand Strategy
Identity and Art Direction

Everyday Sunday
Brand Strategy, Identity and Packaging Design

Everyday Sunday
Brand Strategy, Identity and Packaging Design

DAVID SIMMONDS PHOTOGRAPHER

lightlinespace.com | simmonds.com.au

Iconic Melbourne - Shrine
Client Silver Top Taxi Service

Iconic Melbourne - St Kilda Boulevard
Client Silver Top Taxi Service

Fine art photography for corporate interiors and branding, expressing your company's identity and core values. For your working and living spaces, or just because you love it.

For over a decade David's artistic eye has been creating extraordinary beauty out of our urban and natural environments. Transforming our world into works that lift hearts, open minds, even have us "looking skywards, knowing no bounds", our breath taken away.

Select images from our extensive catalogue, or ask David and Sandra to create a unique work that tells your story, reflecting your goals and achievements. Our images, carefully crafted, superbly printed and presented will enhance your space and your life for years to come.

Corporate Cathedral
Client McLean Delmo Bentleys

DELOITTE DIGITAL

deloittedigital.com

Animated LED screens for L'Oreal
Video, Melbourne Fashion Festival

beconsumed.southaustralia.com
Microsite
South Australian Tourism Commission

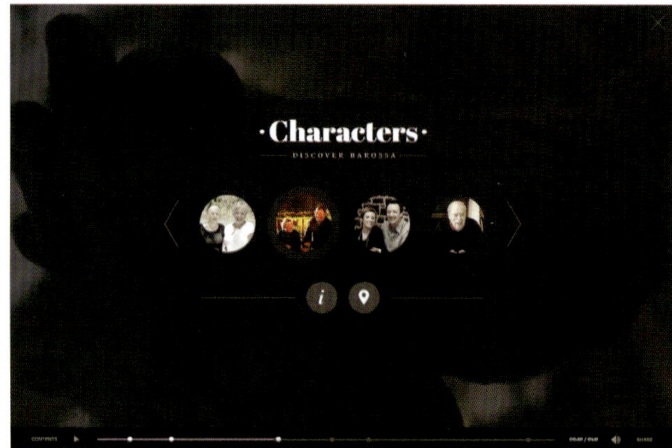

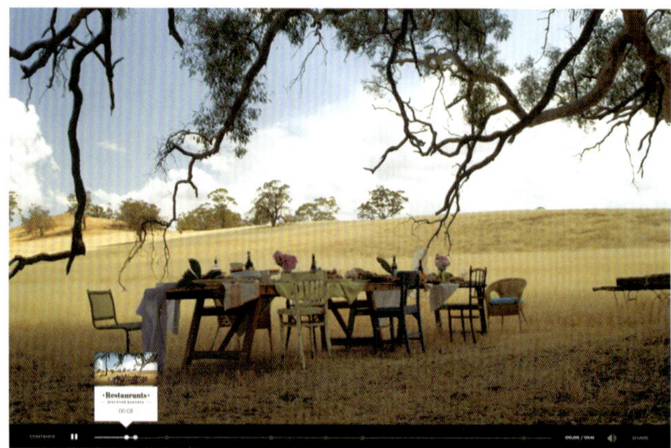

Part Business. Part Creative. Part Technology. One hundred per cent digital. Pioneered in Australia, Deloitte Digital is committed to helping clients unlock the business value of emerging technologies. Through studios spread across six countries, we provide clients with a full suite of digital services, covering digital strategy, user experience, content, creative, engineering and implementation across mobile, web and social media channels. Deloitte Digital brings many different perspectives to our clients' challenges and opportunities, combining an established footprint in mobile, web, ecommerce, social and content management with the strength of our global network of digital studios.

Animated screens and Info bar app for ANZ
Concept Branch

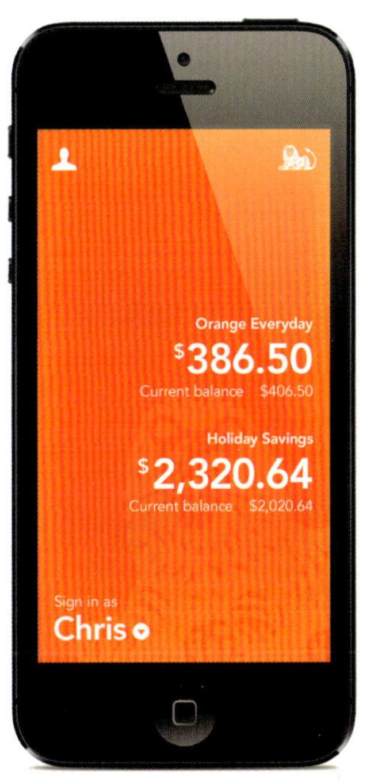

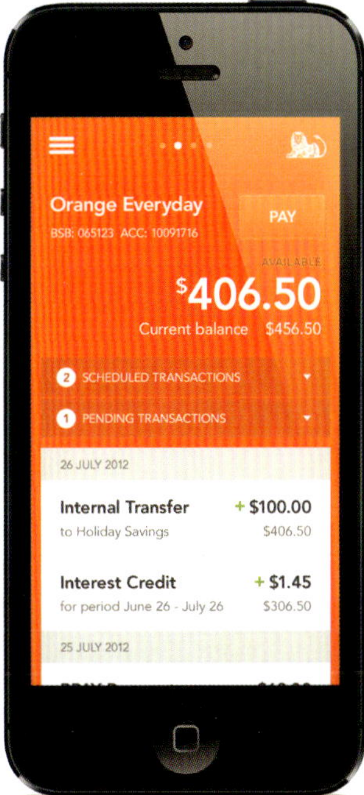

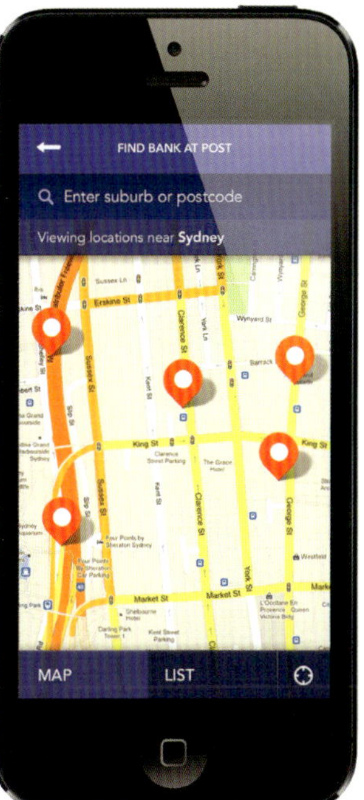

Creative design for ING Direct
Mobile Application

DIADEM

diadem.com.au

Hightpoint Shopping Centre Wayfinding
Wayfinding solution to suit long term objectives

Giant Bikes Store, Hampton
Reinvigorate the in-store experience

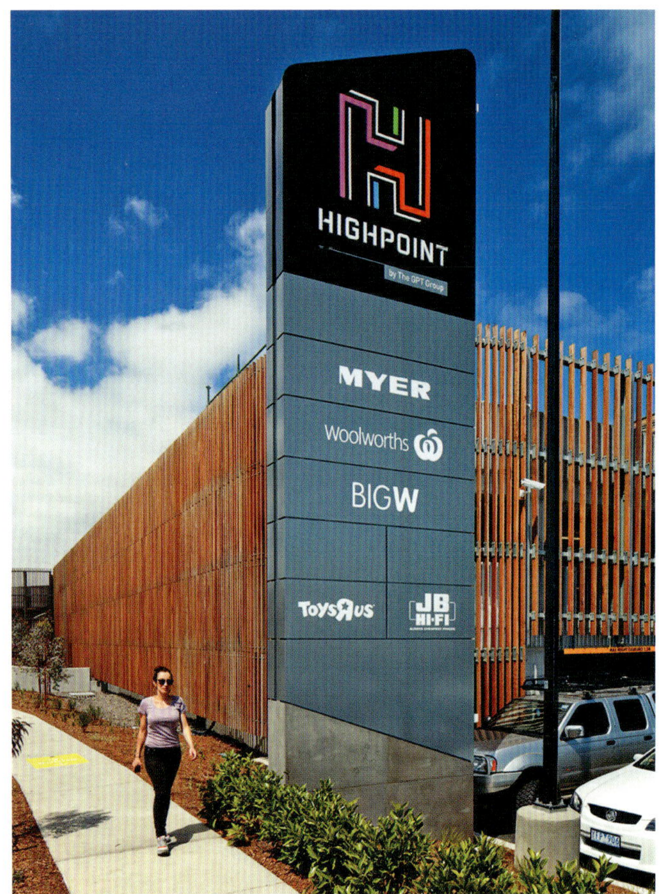

Diadem's primary purpose is to help creative agencies and clients enable design that creates positive customer experiences in the built environment.

At Diadem we encourage progressive thinking, passion and the pursuit of all things new. With focus and purpose we challenge convention and strive for creative excellence.

We believe innovation that works holds most value and delivers certainty for our clients.

We believe in thinking differently. Good design, clear communication and quality delivery translate to improved customer experiences, consistent branding and better project results.

Our aim is simple - to explore possibilities and deliver smarter outcomes.

Environmental Installation, Woods Bagot
Range of installations & environmental graphics

DROGA5

droga5.com.au

Made by MOG
Juice Bottle Design

Qantus, Round the world fare
Poster campaign

Qantas, DM campaign
A set of 10 books edited
to suit Qantas' key flights

At Droga 5 we describe ourselves as creatively led and strategically driven.

Others have described us as category-defying and category-creating.

We believe in consistently asking the hardest questions and delivering the most audacious answers to help to build some of the biggest brands in Australia and beyond.

We also believe that, whatever the problem, not every solution is an advertising campaign.

Here are examples of recent work that didn't follow the traditional paths.

LYNX campaign 'Play'
Pack Design

Dry Dock
Poster Campaign

FUTUREBRAND

futurebrand.com.au | futurebrand.com

Brand identity and Design, Brand strategy incl. Brand architecture, Naming, Innovation, Employer of choice, Internal engagement, Brand governance, Corporate identity, Packaging design, Digital Asset management, Environment

We are the creative future company. We work collaboratively with our clients to create the future for their brand and their business through creative and strategic consultancy. Future brands are always built on a powerful idea, which comes to life across every aspect of the brand experience.

We have helped create, revitalise and redefine some of Australia's most compelling, valuable and loved brands as well as working with leading global brands.

MELBOURNE
FESTIVAL

GET STARTED

getstarted.com.au

Curve, Mobile Industrial Design Magazine
Responsive Website

Deakin University, Student Association Portal
Responsive Website

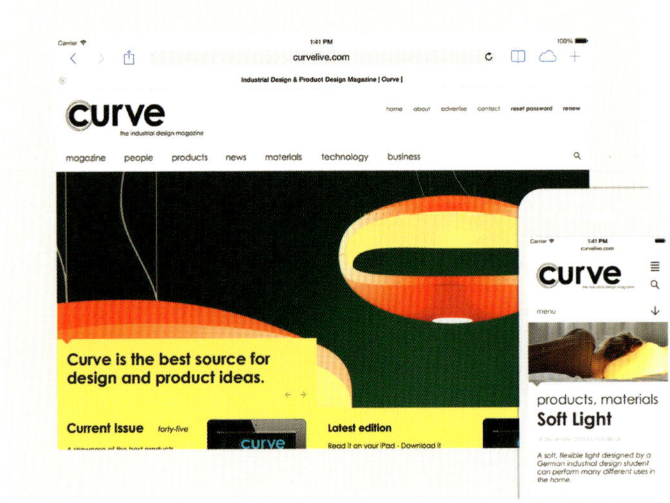

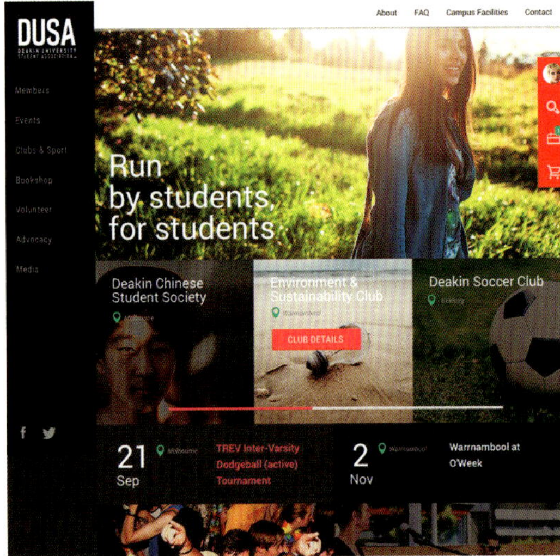

Get Started is proud to have been creating digital experiences since 1999. With a portfolio that includes some the of biggest names in Australian government, retail and corporate, our knowledge and understanding of digital strategy is unmatched within the market. This expertise, mixed with a superior client engagement model breaks the mould. Core company values ensure every project delivers a digital experience that matters – to the client, to their audience and to the Get Started team.

Whether it's a site refresh, going mobile, extending into ecommerce or creating a fully responsive digital experience, we will craft an approach that fits your brand and delivers to your organisational objectives. Allow Get Started to Create Digital Experiences for you.

Snooze, Bedding and Furniture Shopping Experience
Responsive Website

GLOBAL CREATURE TECHNOLOGY

creaturetechnology.com

King Kong
Theatre
Photo James Morgan

How To Train Your Dragon
Arena Show
Photo Jeff Bushby

Walking With Dinosaurs
Arena Show
Photo David Scheinmann

Global Creature Technology designs and produces the most technologically sophisticated, creatively inspired and life-like animatronic creatures for arena spectaculars, theme parks, exhibitions and stage shows in the world.

An extraordinary team of artisans, engineers and designers operating from a non-descript factory in West Melbourne began in 2006 by creating full-scale naturalistic dinosaurs for Walking with Dinosaurs – The Arena Spectacular, a show now seen by over 7 million people in 200 cities around the world. How to Train Your Dragon – The Arena Spectacular for DreamWorks followed and then King Kong which stunned audiences in Melbourne before heading global.

Visit creaturetechnology.com or follow us on Facebook to keep up to date with more amazing projects that are in the works.

HACKETT FILMS

hackettfilms.com

'Choose Your Own Adventure' TVC
National Maritime Museum

ABC TV Tractor Monkeys
Broadcast Package

At Hackett Films we've built a reputation for original, entertaining character animation and design-driven storytelling.

From the deadly serious to the wickedly silly, we've tackled everything from television commercials to children's apps, with a simple goal of keeping the audience always coming back for more.

Established in 2004, Hackett Films has grown to be one of Sydney's prominent production studios specializing in all forms of animation and motion graphics including live action.

Storytelling and innovation are the driving forces behind Hackett Films as we strive to deliver high production value across a variety of media and platforms.

GOZER

gozer.com.au

India Unbound
Website Design

The Big Issue
Magazine Art Direction and design

Stephanie Alexander
Identity, branding, digital

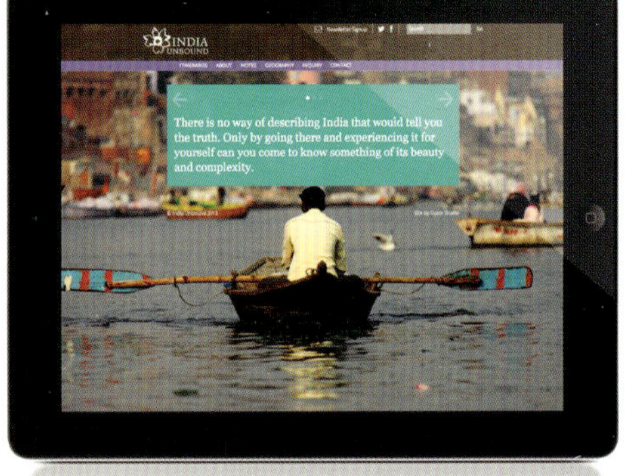

DESIGN – DIGITAL – MOTION

Gozer is a multidisciplinary studio providing a wealth of creative and technical services.

As a graphic design studio we focus on beautiful, bespoke branding.

As a digital agency we provide solid, reliable solutions.

As a production/post-production facility we possess a full suite of services to best tell your story.

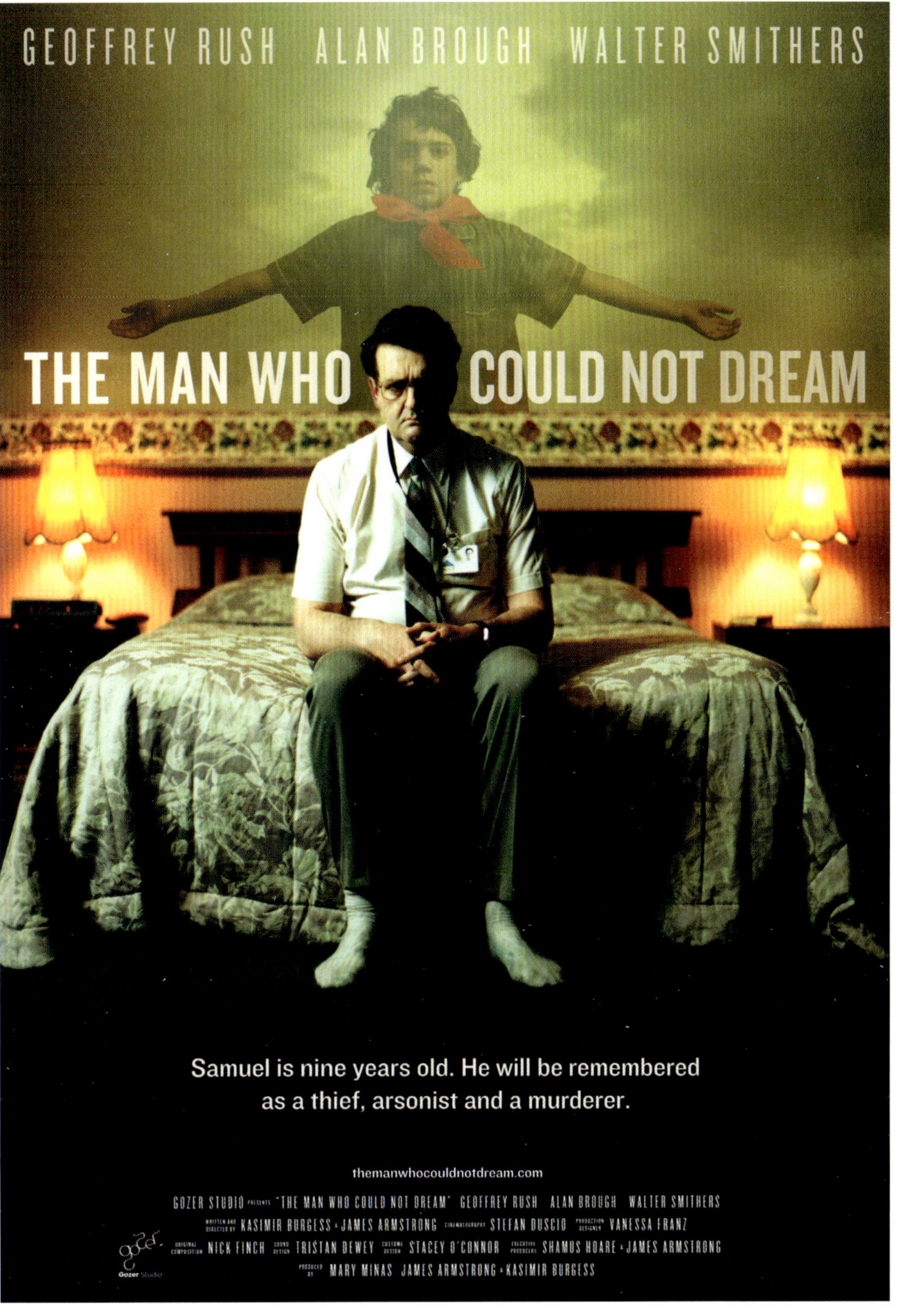

The Man Who Could Not Dream
Self-produced short film

HARCUS DESIGN

harcus.com.au

The Good Food Co
Brand identity

Jansz Tasmania
Wine packaging and gift boxes

Yalumba, The Guardian
Wine packaging

At Harcus Design we create and deliver quality, impactful design solutions that work for our clients, making their products and services shine.

Over 30 years, we have developed a reputation nationally and internationally for excellence in creative thinking and its successful realisation.

Visual identity, brand collateral, three dimensional work – both packaging and environmental – and building long-lasting client relationships are among our fortes.

Maine Beach Ligurian Honey
Body and beauty packaging

HOYNE

hoyne.com.au

Publication design
George & Allen

Sales suite design
George & Allen

Branding
George & Allen

Hoyne is recognised as Australia's most effective brand agency. For us – making an impact is what counts.

Increasing market share, boosting sales and changing perceptions are how we add value.

From offices in Melbourne and Sydney, we do this creatively, strategically and without smoke and mirrors; speaking in a language our clients can understand, working with a genuine passion to achieve the very best.

Identity for new BorrowBox app
Bolinda

BORROW FOR
ADVENTURE

Borrow
Box.
Designed and powered
by Bolinda digital

Get it now

Borrow, download and enjoy ebooks and
eaudiobooks with BorrowBox Library app.

BorrowBox poster design
Bolinda

HUGH PEACHEY

hughpeachey.com

Smoking Girl
The laneway series
Personal project

Hugh Peachey has been delivering evocative commercial photography for over 15 years. He is self-represented in Melbourne and has a Sydney and Singapore agent. His work has been featured on major campaigns for companies such as Nike, Telstra, Worksafe and Ambra.

His photography is always highly considered, sometimes off-beat, sometimes quirky. Hugh is very 'particular' and is well-renowned for his skillful use of lighting techniques that clearly define his photography. His work has a raw humanist approach – where he sensitively explores his subject. Needless to say his portraiture is often other-worldly.

As Hugh continues to push boundaries and explore the photographic realm he has recently begun working as a DOP and is now filming TVC's and online content.

Runaway
The laneway series
Personal project

PAPER STONE SCISSORS

paperstonescissors.com

Fresh Food Spring/Summer Campaign 2013
Highpoint Shopping Centre
Concept, Art Direction, Design and Production

Peter Alexander Season Campaign 2013
Concept, Art Direction, Design and Production

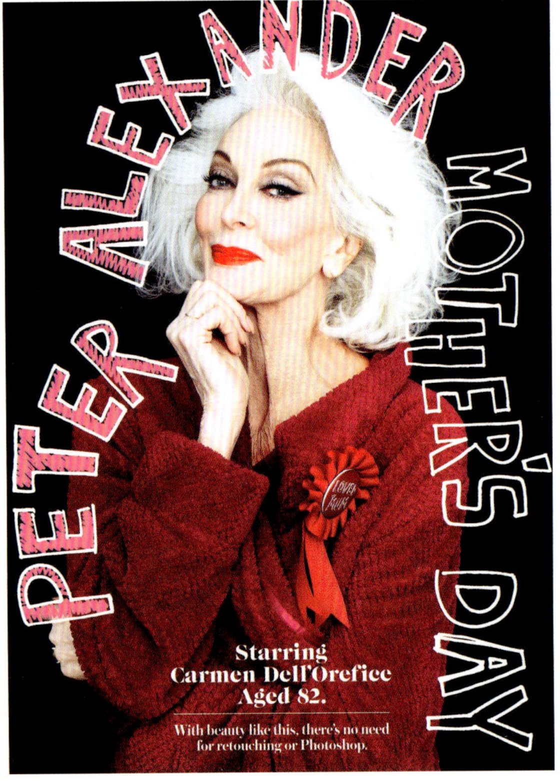

Paper Stone Scissors is a global communications agency helping brands to set the pace for change. We do this through multi-channel communications that are always consistent, concise and engaging.

We work across the full range of organisations from Australia's largest shopping malls to China's fastest growing women's retailer to small start ups looking to secure a place in the market.

Our fingerprint touches household brand names from luxury to fast fashion.

We are made up of specialists across a wide range of disciplines, from art directors, designers, digital strategists and producers.

Company Profile 2013, McKellar Renown Press
Concept, Art Direction, Design and Production

BRIAN SADGROVE DESIGN

sadgrove.com

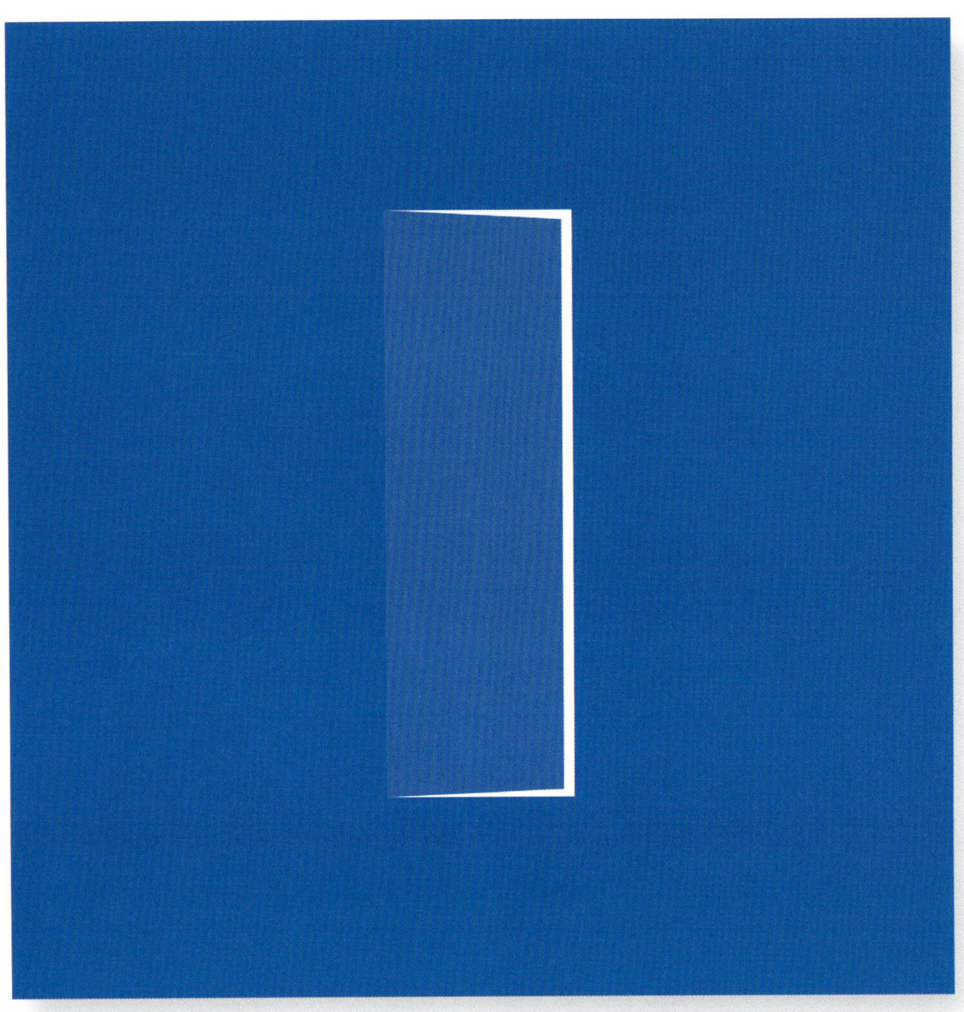

KANDAN

kandan.com.au

Ambient
Infiniti sponsorship
Cirque du Soleil 'OVO

3D Drink Coasters
Cirque VIP bar

3D Display Wall
Infiniti Sponsorship
Cirque du Soleil 'OVO'

Kandan is not a design agency. It's not an advertising agency. It's not a digital agency. It's is not an activation agency. It incorporates elements of all these.

We are an agency that puts our clients, and their success, at the heart of everything we do. We bring brands to life and create ideas that surprise and we deliver results.

We are hard working and driven toward producing great ideas. Being able to implement the ideas in a way that evokes interest and ultimately gets results is a rarity.

At Kandan we think about the end result each step of the way to bring ideas to life in the most effective way possible.

SAVI

savi.com.au

STK
Outdoor advertising
Brochure Cover
Promotional Kit
Caydon

10 years. 140 Savi Brands.

Design and creative solutions to align brands, media and audience. Spanning multiple disciplines across varied platforms, we use current and emerging technology to turn insights into action. Innovatively led, our strategy is articulate, direct and agile.

Our creative communication is with purpose, to accelerate business and engage audiences in a relevant and authentic way. Our approach is customised and the result of ongoing client collaboration, our process is backed by research and extensive experience.

We deliver content to start conversations and drive consumer response. Communicating a brand's unique story ensures distinction and clarity in a noisy marketplace.

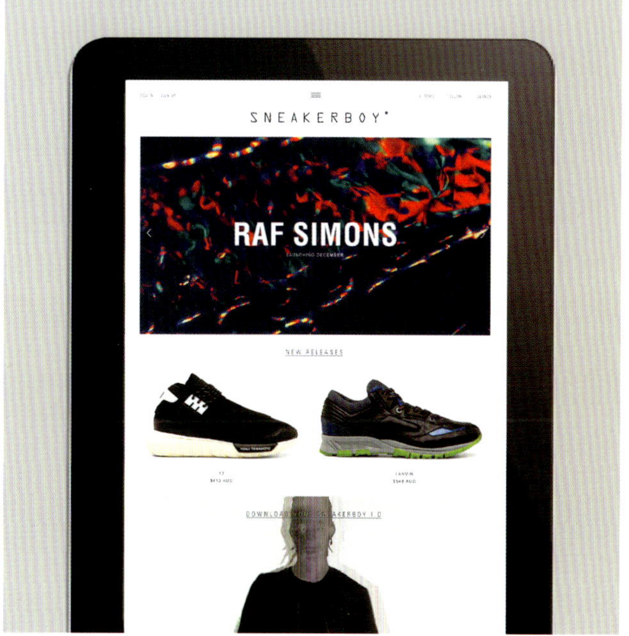

Bloom
Outdoor Advertising
Press Advertising
Five Squared

Sneakerboy
Mobile App
Webstore Design

SECTOR7G MAKING BRANDS VISIBLE

sector7g.com.au

Australian Fabians
Progressive political think tank
Brand mark

Hedone
Indie film production company
Visual Identity

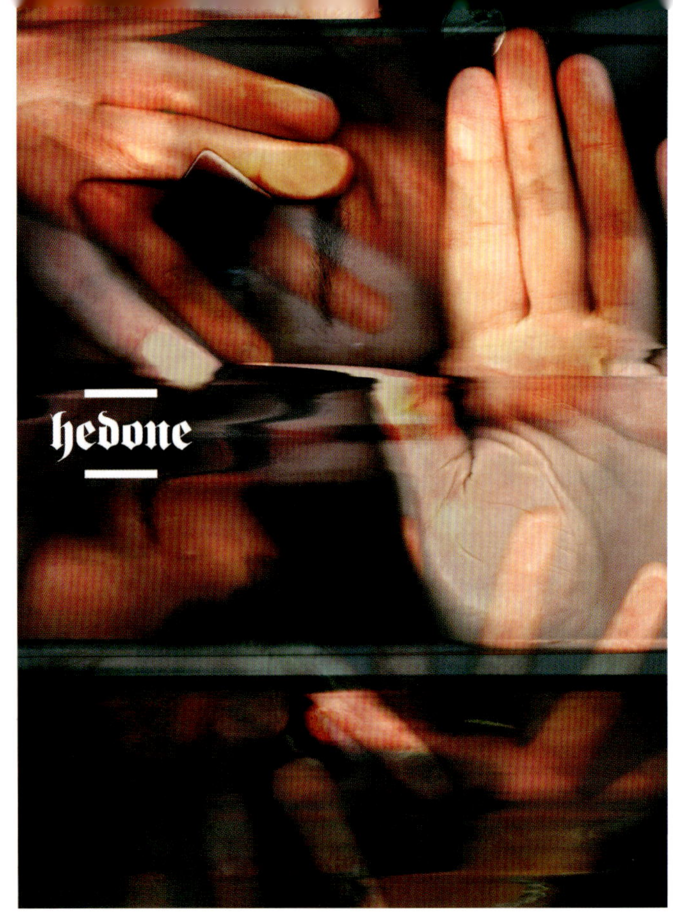

Australian Fabians.

We are a visual communication studio that specialises in delivering high-impact graphic design supported by sound marketing principals.

Our credo is that good design is defined by clarity of communication, distinction of ideas and attention to detail.

We like to think before we make and we like to challenge the preconceived notions of where a brand can go. Our expertise is in brand design and visual identity systems for business.

We also work on environmental graphics, signage, websites, publication design and packaging.

Music Amplifies my life
AGDA Australian Poster Biennale 2012
Poster

Madderns, Intellectual Property Firm
Brand book cover

SHABBADU

shabbadu.com.au

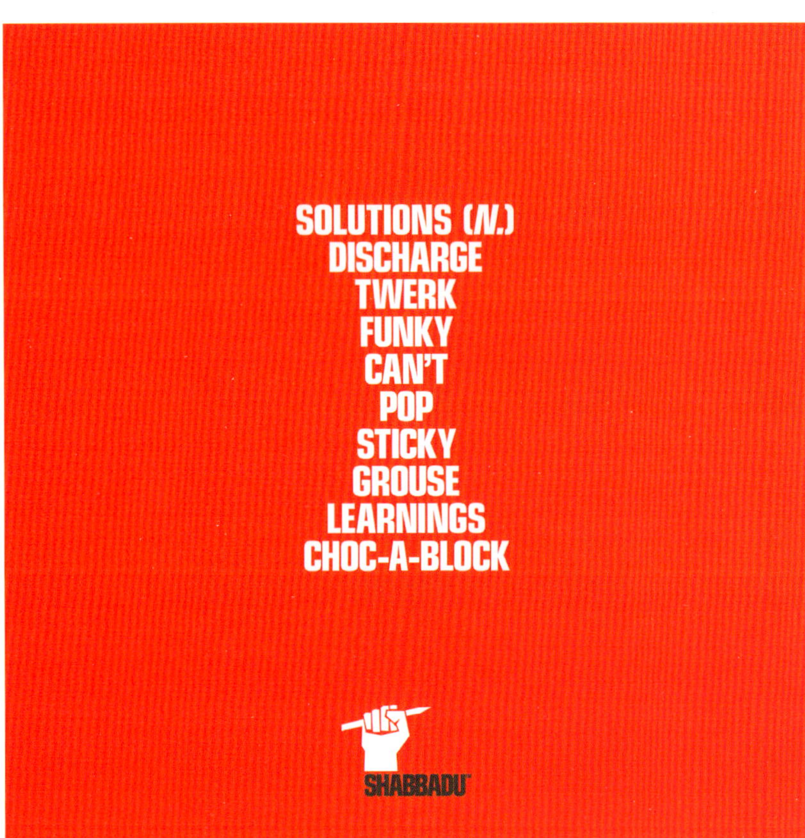

Shabbadu are a specialist copywriting, strategy and concept development agency. So what are we doing tucked deep inside the back pocket of one of the world's most prestigious design organisations' design directory? Well, it just so happens that we've been the Official Supplier of Words to agIdeas for the past two years.

So instead of trying to compete with the beautifully designed, fastidiously crafted layouts surrounding us, we thought we'd give you an insight into what we're like by listing some of our favourite and least favourite words. We hope you find them equally enlightening and vexatious.

CURMUDGEONLY
OBSTREPEROUS
RETICULATED
WONDERFUL
WISP
YES
QUIVER
TREMENDOUS
CONQUISTADOR
HABERDASHERY

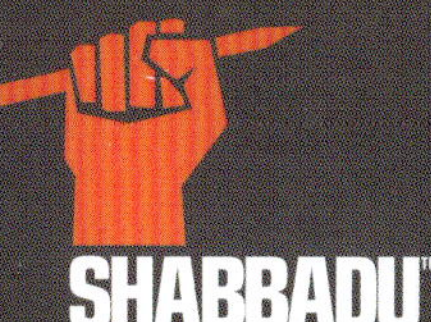

SHABBADU™

SONIA PAYES

soniapayes.com.au

Installation
Exhibition Interzone, 2013
Fehily Contemporary, Melbourne

Interzone #6, #7, #8,
C-type print, 2013
6mm Acrylic mount, 72 x 72cm

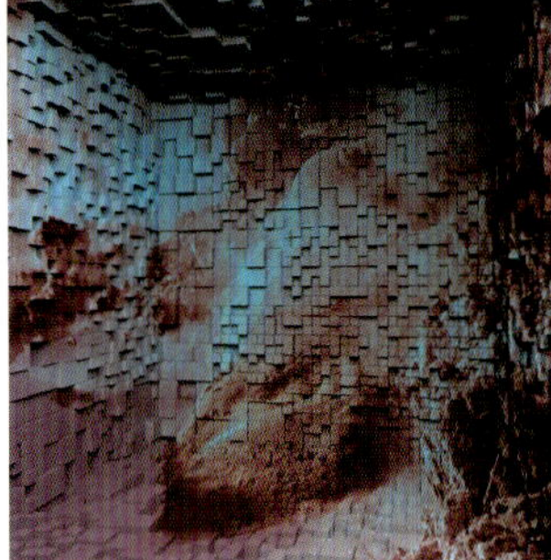

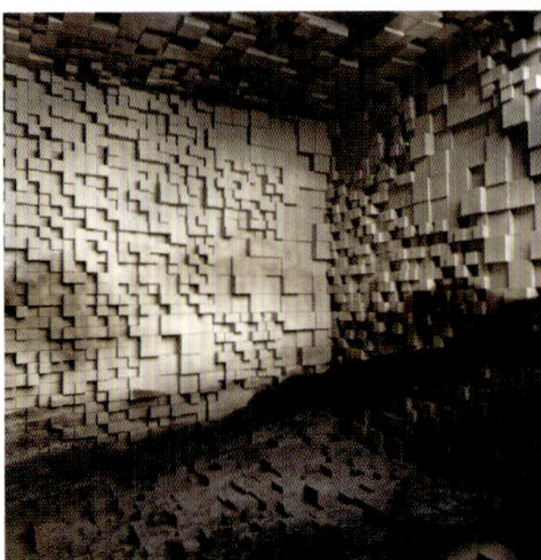

Sonia Payes is an internationally acclaimed photographer and new media artist based in Melbourne. Payes' work veers towards the surreal. Haunting portraits and landscapes that reveal layers of meaning and intent, with things inverted, overlaid, obscured and left unseen. Working with multi-media animations and 3D installations is a new aspect of her practice that provides unlimited potential to explore the largely environmental themes of destruction, apocalypse and renewal. Payes has recently exhibited in China, New Zealand and Australia. Her works are held in major public collections including the National Gallery of Victoria, Jewish Museum of Australia, Monash Gallery of Art, McClelland Gallery + Sculpture Park, and many private collections throughout Australia and overseas. Payes is represented by Fehily Contemporary, Melbourne.

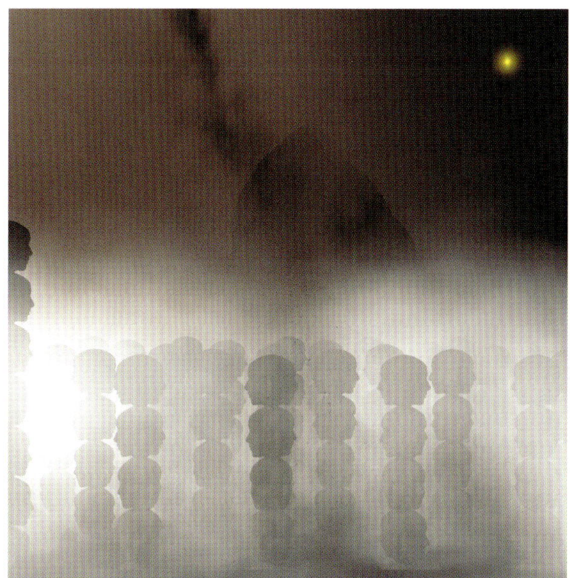

Corn and quarries
3D animation - 3 minutes, 2013

Interzone #9, #10
C-type print, 2013
6mm Acrylic mount, 72 x 72cm each

UNO

uno.net.au

De Oko Melkburen, Organic Milk
Packaging & Branding

Laboratory Sampling Robot, ePrep
Product Design & Branding

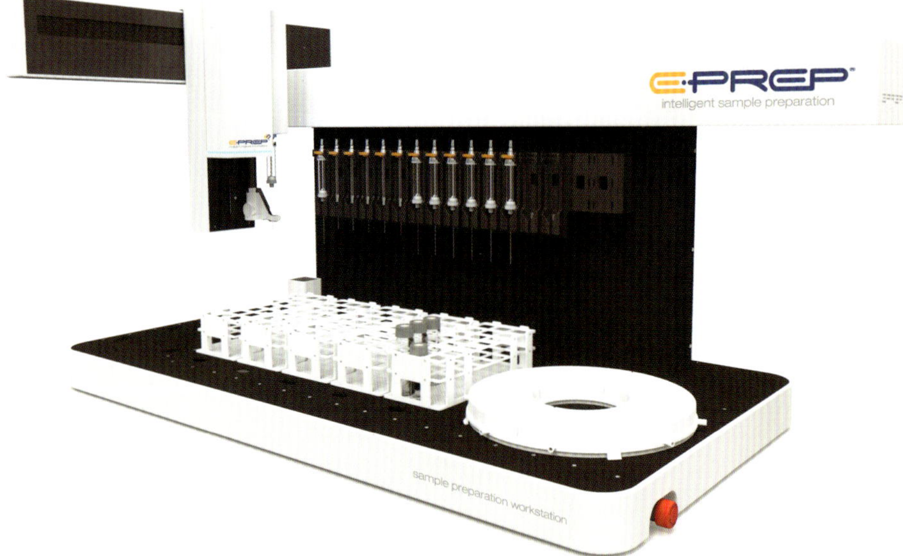

UNO Australia is a team of professionals from different design backgrounds who all posses the ability to think outside the square.

The group diversity enables us to visualize new directions, develop solutions to complex problems, challenge and drive change whilst delivering tangible benefits to all stakeholders and a 'return-on-investment' to our clients.

The entire UNO team interacts to ensure branding, packaging design, product development, retail design, interior architecture and project delivery are seamlessly brought together to create outstanding results through design.

See Inside.. Think Outside...

Dulux World of Colour
Retail Architecture, Exhibition Design
designEX

Herbivore Veggie Bar
Hospitality and Branding Design

XYZ STUDIOS

xyzstudios.com

Invincible, Frank Health Insurance
Animation TVC

Incarceration, Sesame Workshop
Animation Online

Overslept, Acer
Animation TVC

XYZ is home to exceptional directors who mix design, illustration, animation, visual effects and live action to lead avant-garde commercial works from conceptual development through to final delivery.

Numbers, ING Direct
Animation TVC

PREMIER'S DESIGN AWARDS

PREMIER'S DESIGN AWARDS

PREMIER'S
DESIGN
AWARDS

Good design can also be the difference between treading water and prospering in an increasingly competitive global economy. Design accounts for an estimated $204 million in exports and $7.3 billion annually to Victoria's economy.

Highlighting the economic, environmental and social benefits of investing in good design, the prestigious Premier's Design Awards celebrate and reward both designers and firms for excellence in the development and use of design.

Building on last year's awards, the 2013 awards program recognises and celebrates diversity in design with the inclusion of six award categories. The ward categories are: Architectural Design, Service Design, Product Design, Communication Design, Digital Design and Design Strategy.

For the second year, Victorian design icon, Ken Cato AO, chaired the judging panel made up of prominent Australian and international experts – reflecting the breadth and depth of the design industry and design application.

The judging panel brings together a wealth of diverse design perspectives to judge the application, as well as strengthening the national and international profile of the awards. The Victorian Government is committed to driving best practice design in Victoria, growing awareness of design, building business capability and fostering excellence in design skills, through the delivery of the $10 million Victorian Design Initiatives 2012–15.

GOOD DESIGN MEANS TAKING FIVE MINUTES TO EXIT A CROWDED SPORTS STADIUM INSTEAD OF FIFTEEN. IT'S AN INDUSTRIAL STRENGTH LADDER THAT IS STILL EASY TO MANOEUVRE. IT'S THE ELIMINATION OF DOUBLE-HANDLING DATA ENTERED ONLINE. DESIGN CAN RE-INVIGORATE YOUR BUSINESS AND GIVE YOU A CRITICAL COMPETITIVE EDGE.

JUDGING CRITERIA

DESIGN EXCELLENCE:
Effective use of professional design to solve a legitimate problem or need, or to create an opportunity.

Degree of functional and aesthetic appeal to a broad range of users.

DESIGN TRANSFORMATION:
Degree of design-led transformation i.e. how has the investment in professional design transformed the client's business.

Extent to which design is now integrated in the client's processes and activities.

DESIGN IMPACT:
Impact of the product on the client's business performance i.e. market share, financial sustainability, environmental and social outcomes.

Impact of industry and end-user adoption of the design.

DESIGN INNOVATION:
Original design concepts and insights or ways of design thinking that enhance the user's experience.

Degree of cross-disciplinary design and its impact on enabling innovation, productivity and sets new standards or benchmarks.

KEN CATO, AO CHAIRMAN CAT
OF THE PREMIER'S DESIGN AW
PORCINI, USA CHIEF DESIGN O
BARRATT, USA PRESIDENT AI
PEARCE, UK PARTNER, PENTA
NSW FOUNDER AND PRINCIPAL
CHRIS DOYLE, NSW FOUNDER,
MARK ARMSTRONG, NSW CO-
GROUP, MANFRED WANG, TAIW
OFFICER BENQ & QISDA CORPO
NSW DIRECTOR OF DESIGN AN
GABRIELA RODRIGUEZ, MEXIC

O PARTNERS CHAIRMAN
VARDS JUDGING PANEL, MAURO
FFICER AT PEPSICO, JOHN
ID CEO AT TEAGUE, HARRY
GRAM LONDON, JANE STARK,
DESIGNER AT STARK DESIGN,
CHRISTOPHER DOYLE & CO,
FOUNDER BLUE SKY DESIGN
VAN VP & CHIEF DESIGN
RATION, RICHARD HOARE,
D INNOVATION BREVILLE GROUP,
O DIRECTOR AT VERDMX

DESIGN STRATEGY

Nike+Nine

Designed by: Local Peoples

Commissioned by: Nike

DESIGN STRATEGY

ARCHITECTURAL DESIGN

Box Hill Gardens Multi Use Purpose Area
Designed by: ASPECT Studios & NMBW
Architecture Studio
Commissioned by: Whitehorse City Council

Crumpler Prahran
Designed by: Russell & George
Commissioned by: Crumpler

FabPod
Designed by: Spatial Information Architecture Laboratory (SIAL), RMIT University
Commissioned by: RMIT University, Property Services

Fairhaven Beach House
Designed by: John Wardle Architects
Commissioned by: Arnold Thomas Becker

ARCHITECTURAL DESIGN

Footscray Nicholson Learning Commons
Designed by: Cox Architecture
Commissioned by: Victoria University

Headquarters for Birkenstock Australia
Designed by: Melbourne Design Studios (Architecture)
Commissioned by: Birkenstock Australia

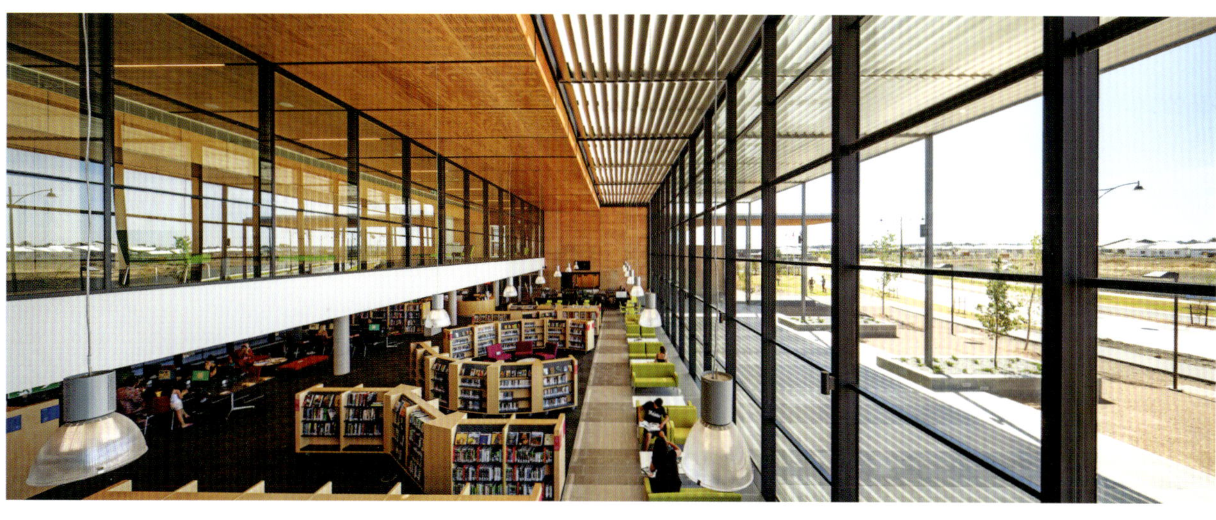

Hume Global Learning Centre & Library – Craigieburn
Designed by: fjmt (Francis-Jones Morehen Thorp)
Commissioned by: Manager Projects & Contract Management

Luna
Designed by: Callum Fraser
Commissioned by: Buxton Group

ARCHITECTURAL DESIGN

ARCHITECTURAL DESIGN

Mildura Eco Living Centre
Designed by: EME Design Pty Ltd
Commissioned by: Mildura Rural City Council

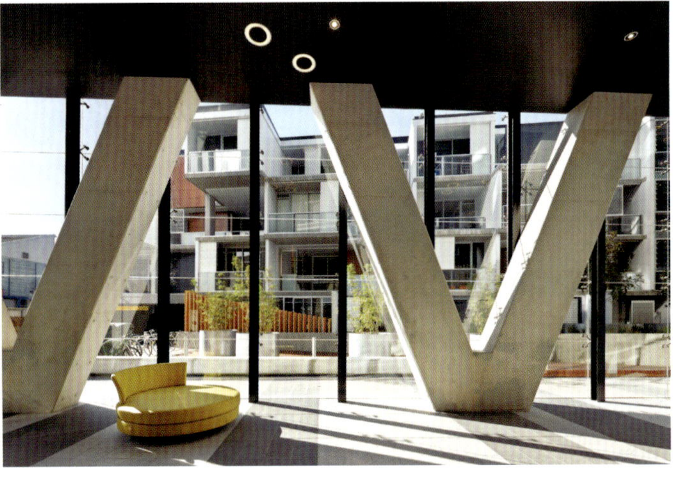

Roi Apartments
Designed by: Bird de la Coeur Architects
Commissioned by: Rare City Acre

South Morang Rail Extension
Designed by: Cox Architecture
Commissioned by: Public Transport Victoria

The Australian Garden Completion
Designed by: Taylor Cullity Lethlean with Paul Thompson
Commissioned by: Royal Botanic Gardens

COMMUNICATION DESIGN

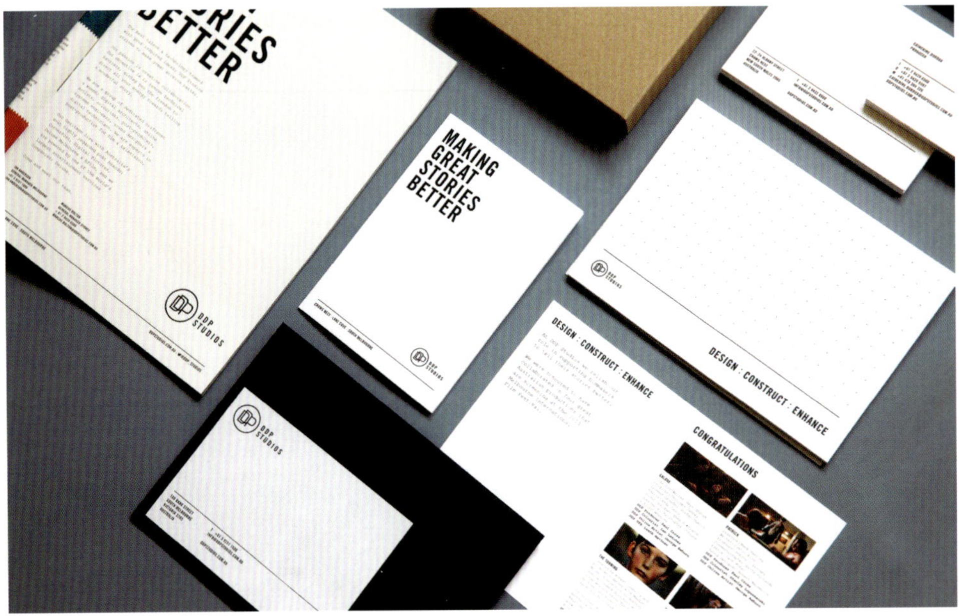

DDP Studios Brand
Designed by: Aer Design
Commissioned by: Deluxe Entertainment Services Group Australia

DULUX World of Colour Exhibit – designEX 2013
Designed by: UNO Australia
Commissioned by: Dulux Australia

Gifts of Change Brand Review and Marketing Campaign
Designed by: Thatworks
Commissioned by: International Women's Development Agency Inc.

Mayver's Rebrand
Designed by: Saltree
Commissioned by: Health Farm Fine Foods

COMMUNICATION DESIGN

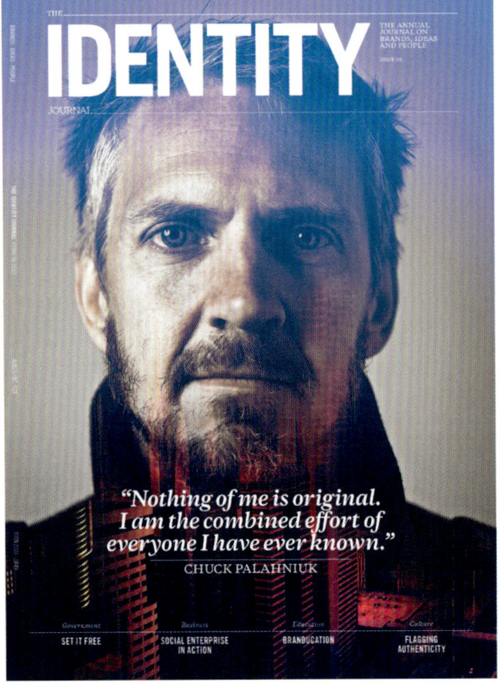

The Identity Journal
Designed by: TANK Branding
Commissioned by: TANK Branding

The World Stamp Expo
Designed by: Australia Post
Commissioned by: Australia Post

Assemble Papers
Designed by: Content and Design direction by Assemble
Commissioned by: Assemble

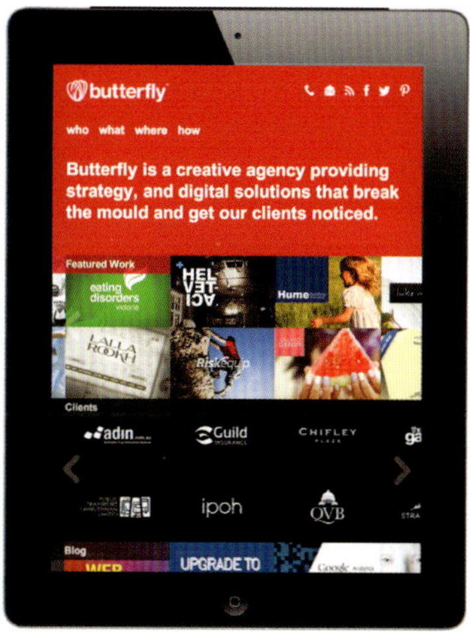

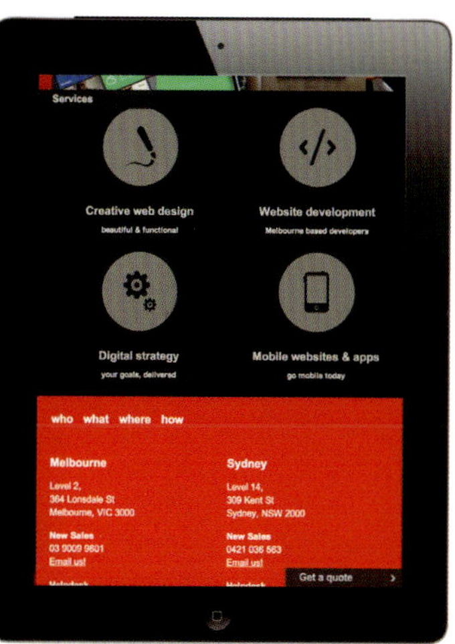

Butterfly Responsive website www.butterfly.com.au
Designed by: Butterfly
Commissioned by: Butterfly

DIGITAL DESIGN

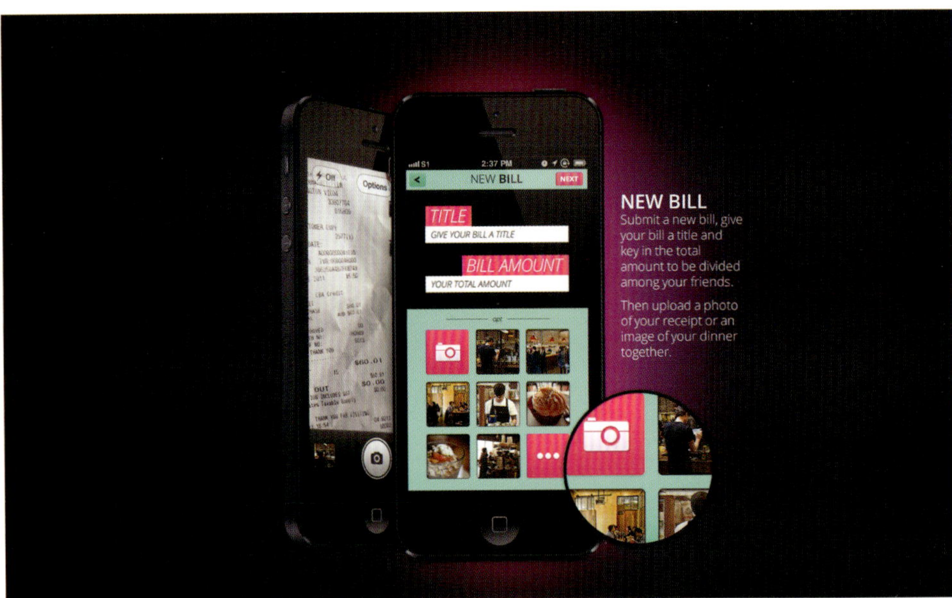

Go Dutch!
Designed by: Studioee
Commissioned by: Syn-Ee Wong

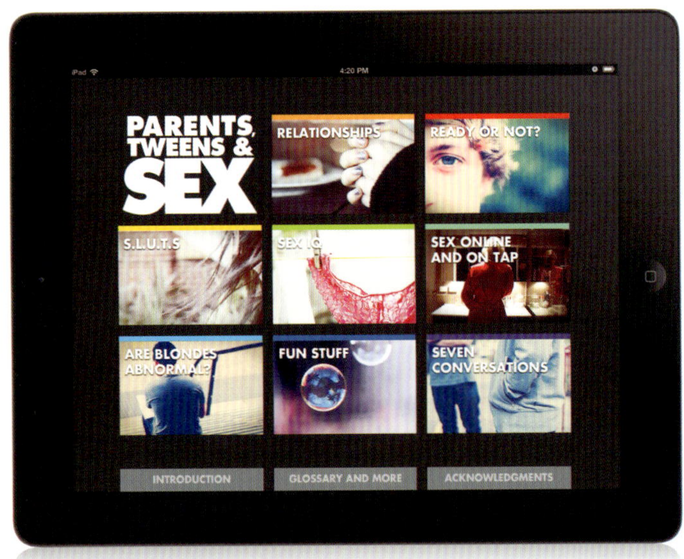

Parents, Tweens & Sex
Designed by: Faculty of Design, Swinburne University of Technology
Commissioned by: Action Psychology

Telstra.com Consumer Site Redesign

Designed by: Telstra Digital

Cmmissioned by: Telstra Digital

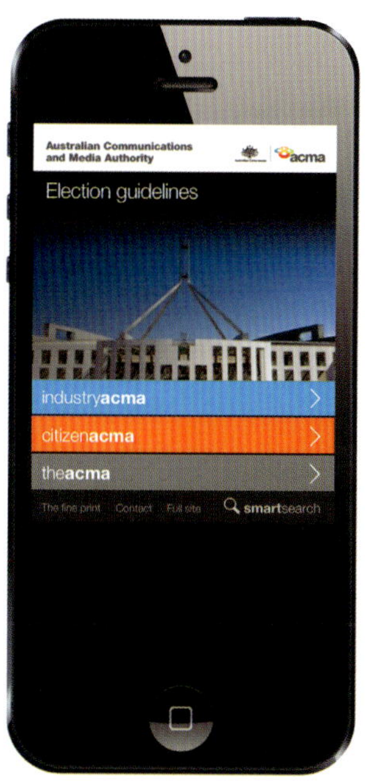

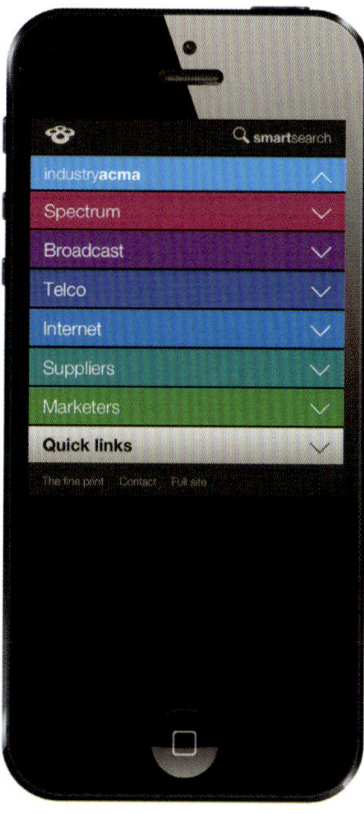

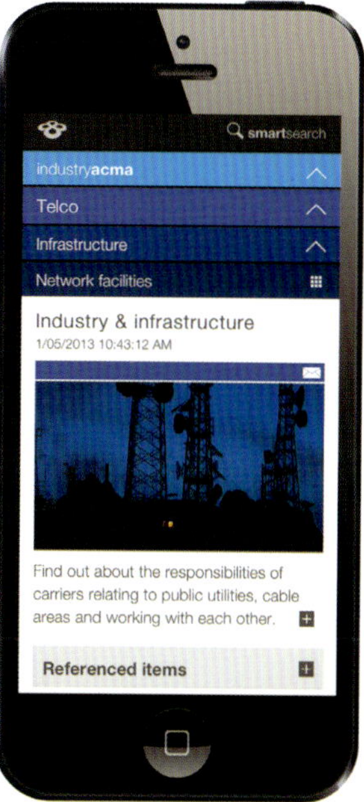

The ACMA Website

Designed by: Aer Design

Commissioned by: Australian Communications and Media Authority

DIGITAL DESIGN

UniFORM
Designed by: Evado
Commissioned by: Evado Pty Ltd

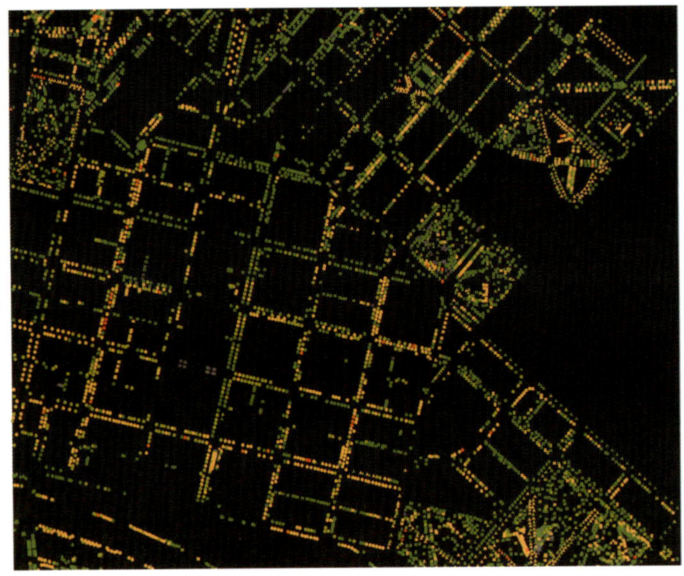

Visualising Melbourne's Urban Forest
Designed by: OOM Creative
Commissioned by: City of Melbourne

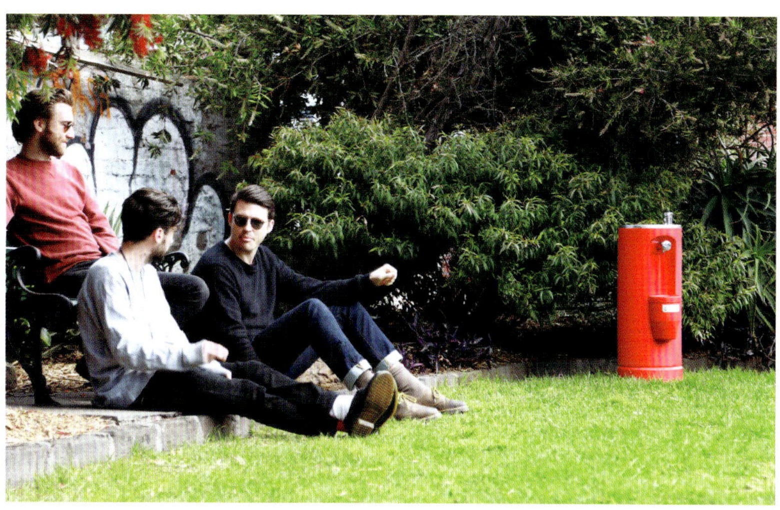

aquaBUBBLER drinking fountain with water bottle refill station
Designed by: Waterford Trading Pty Ltd
Commissioned by: Waterford Trading Pty Ltd

b.box Essential Baby Bottle
Designed by: b.box for kids
Commissioned by: BBox for Kids Development Pty Ltd

PRODUCT DESIGN

Backpack Bed™ Tropical
Designed by: Swags for Homeless
Commissioned by: Swags for Homeless

Blackmagic Cinema Camera
Designed by: Blackmagic Industrial Design Team
Commissioned by: Blackmagic Design

Blinder 1 Light
Designed by: Knog Pty Ltd
Commissioned by: Knog Pty Ltd

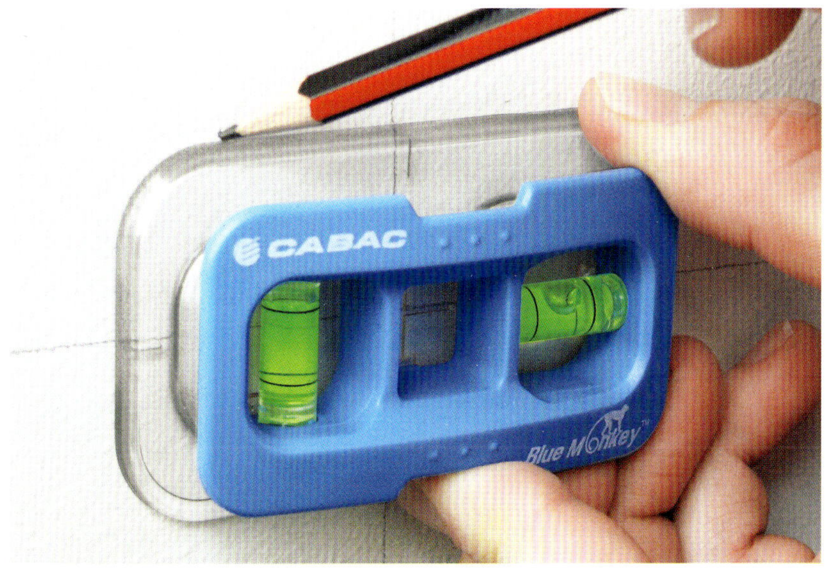

Blue Monkey – Wall Plate Levelling Tool
Designed by: CobaltNiche
Commissioned by: Spears Pacific

PRODUCT DESIGN

BlueAnt Q3 Premium Smartphone Earpiece
Designed by: BlueAnt Wireless
Commissioned by: BlueAnt Wireless

Bombardier E-Class Tram for Melbourne
Designed by: Bombardier
Commissioned by: Bombardier

Concave Quantum1 – Football Boot
Designed by: CobaltNiche
Commissioned by: Concave International

JOMO steel Winged Dish (Mark 2)
Designed by: JOMO Australia
Commissioned by: JOMO Australia

Mandarin 2
Designed by:Toolbox Innovation
Commissioned by: Illumination Solar

Marc Newson Unbreakable Drinkwear
Designed by: Palm Products
Commissioned by: Palm Products

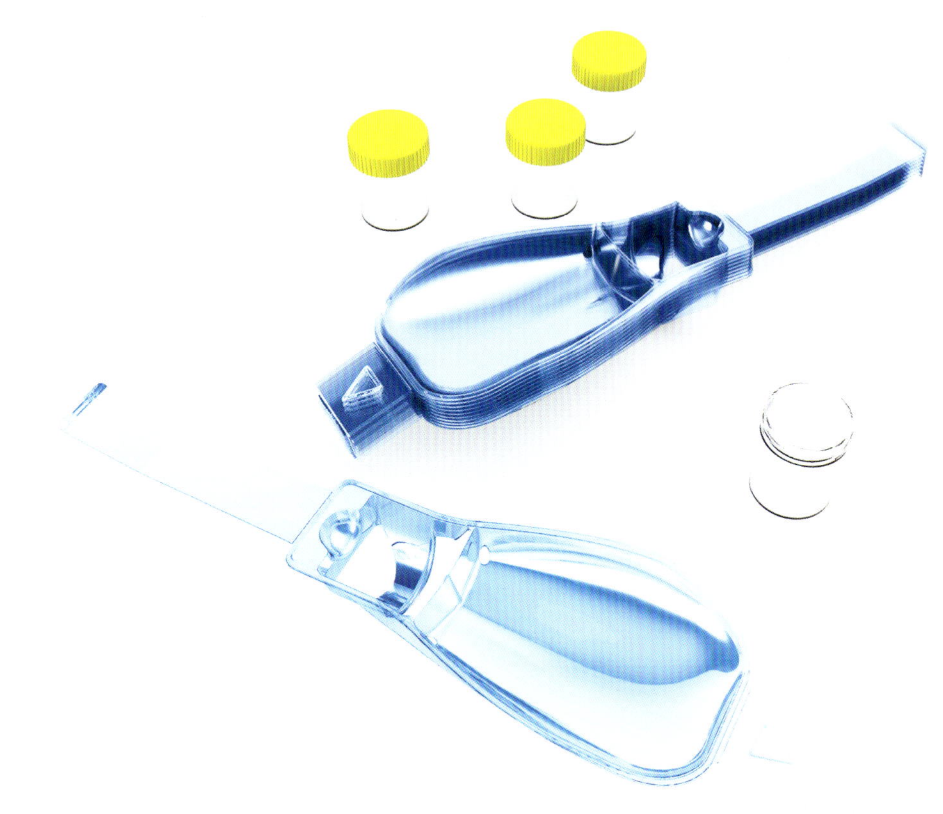

Mittstrom – Mid-Stream Urine Collection Device

Designed by: Fwee Pty Ltd

Commissioned by: Fwee Pty Ltd

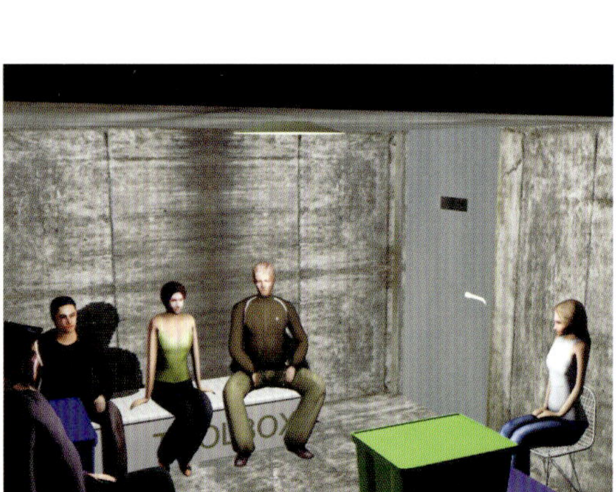

Above-ground Fire Shelters

Designed by: Swinburne University of Technology

Commissioned by: Frankston Concrete Products Pty Ltd

21121Ai 100YC
Designed by: RMIT School of Architecture and Design –
Tom Kovac Director 21121Ai 100YC ECoC
Commissioned by: Maribor European Capital of Culture